A Golden Tear

Danièle Sauvageau's Journey to Olympic Gold

by Sally Manning

Published by

GENERAL STORE
GSPH PUBLISHING HOUSE

Box 28, 1694B Burnstown, Ontario, Canada K0J 1G0
Telephone (613) 432-7697 or 1-800-465-6072

ISBN 1-894263-69-3
Printed and bound in Canada

Layout and design by Derek McEwen
Cover by Taragraphics
Cover photos: Front – CP Picture Archive Kevork Djansezian
             Back – CP Picture Archive Mike Sturk

General Store Publishing House
Burnstown, Ontario, Canada

National Library of Canada Cataloguing in Publication

Manning, Sally, 1949
    A golden tear : Danièle Sauvageau's journey to Olympic gold /
Sally Manning.

ISBN 1-894263-69-3

    1. Sauvageau, Danièle. 2. Women hockey coaches–Canada–
Biography. 3. Winter Olympic Games (19th : 2002 : Salt Lake
City, Utah) I. Title.

GV848.5.S34M35 2002   796.962'092   C2002-905582-2

To Thérèse Croisen Toi
tu as Tous ce
que tu as
Besoin.

Dedicated
to my mom and dad

Acknowledgements

In writing this book, I was presented with my own mountain to climb. Although I picked the route, the actual climb was, by no means, a solo effort. There were many people along the way without whose support, encouragement and assistance I would never have scaled the summit. For this, I must thank them. They are: Danièle Sauvageau, the coach, for tapping the number on my back to jump over the boards in the first place; Tim Gordon, my publisher, who is as passionate as any Canadian about the game we like to call our own; Susan Code McDougall, my editor, for showing me the way; Lou Pamenter, Laura Templeton, Sue Vigneux and Kathy Crandall, all old friends, for caring about me in my new venture; my mom, for always believing in me; my dad, for letting me follow in his footsteps; my brothers, Bob and Jim, and my sisters, Jane, Mary Anne, Nancy and Suzanne, for playing games of all kinds with me; the sport science staff in Calgary who were so patient in answering all my questions; the hockey coaches and administrators who also gave so generously of their time and are a part of the story; Vicky Sunohara, Jayna Hefford, France St-Louis and Louis Robitaille, the "real actors" in the on-ice drama; the RCMP at The Depot and in Powell River for helping me understand what policing is all about; my friend, Wendy Grater for lending me her dining-room table with the view over the lake; and finally, to my good friend, Katja Mathys, for her interest and insights and her keyboarding skills. Without her assistance, the manuscript would still be floating in my head.

Table of Contents

CHAPTER 1

The Game

Responsibility. Determination. Courage.

— Danièle Sauvageau

THE LIVING ROOM on a wintry Saturday night was the setting for some of my fondest childhood memories. The detail is vivid, as if it were yesterday. Mostly, it was my dad in the easy chair and my older brother and me sitting on the well-worn sofa, eyes glued to the box in the corner tuned to Channel 6, the CBC. When the clock struck nine, the musical march of the theme for *Hockey Night in Canada* proclaimed to the nation that Our Game was about to begin. The TV flashed the friendly face of Murray Westgate, immediately recognizable in his ESSO uniform and cap and Pepsodent grin. I always expected to see him step out the station door when our Falcon pulled up to the pumps. Then came the nasal twang of Mr. Hockey himself, Foster Hewitt, announcing his familiar refrain, "Welcome, hockey fans from coast to coast."

On the screen in front of us, the players were swirling around the ice. Although the broadcast was just beginning, the game was already well into the second period. I'd squirm in my seat in anxious anticipation until the scoreboard flashed the fate of my beloved Maple Leafs. Back then, it was still the old six-team league: Toronto, Montreal, Detroit, Boston, New York and Chicago. Our games of shinny on the frozen ponds and rock-hard roads had lineups studded with the heroes we worshipped on our black and white screen: names like Beliveau, Richard, Howe and Mahovlich. My favourite was always Dickie Duff.

Flash forward to February 21, 2002. The clock is approaching 7:00 p.m. Another CBC hockey telecast is about to begin. Once again I am sitting in my living room, this time with a handful of friends waiting patiently for the game to begin. Only, this game is one with a twist. An Olympic game. A gold medal game—Canada versus the U.S.A. The cast of characters is vastly different from the olden days with new names like Wickenheiser, Campbell, Goyette and Sunohara. Their first names—Hayley, Cassie, Danielle and Vicky—affirm this is women's hockey. It has gripped a nation, grabbed it by the throat and won't let go. Seven and a half million viewers in living rooms across the country await the drama about to unfold. Two hours later, a hockey-besotted nation will have a new set of sporting heroes.

On this evening, the atmosphere in the E-Center at Salt Lake City is electric with excitement. With the U.S.A. in the final, the game is a "hot ticket." Scalpers are reaping a bounty, getting up to ten times the face value of a ticket. Canada is going into the game as the underdog, and deservedly so. A year of intensive preparation included eight games against its arch rival, the mighty U.S.A. The record shows eight straight losses. The Americans have steamrolled their foes, undefeated in thirty-five games. Could we turn the tide? So far, the Olympics have been good to us. Four games against lesser opponents—Kazakhstan, Russia, Sweden, Finland—four lopsided victories. Thirty-two goals for, three against. Surely, this means hope for the final. Cassie Campbell, the captain, had said it best: "Forget the others, they don't matter. This is the only one that counts."

At 7:00 p.m. the game begins. The players move cautiously, seeking their rhythm. It reminds me of the first round of a boxing match: the fighters circling the ring, feinting, jabbing, strutting, backpedalling along the ropes, sizing each other up.

First Period. The Two-Minute Mark.

The kid line is on the ice for Canada: Ouellette, Piper, Antal. The faceoff is deep in the American zone. Cherie Piper, a rookie and last-minute addition to the team, follows the draw and nabs the puck behind the end line. In a classic game of cat and mouse, she sweeps around the net and tries to jam the puck between the goalie and the post. The puck ricochets off the pad of DeCosta, the American goalie, and wobbles erratically across the top of the crease where Ouellette, the big right winger, is parked. She swipes at the bouncing black disc, straight lining it into the back of the net. Canada 1, U.S.A. 0.

In the living room we rise as one. "The kid line has done it!" someone whoops. Her teammates mob Ouellette. We high-five each other. "Maybe, just maybe," someone whispers. The players line up at centre ice, the puck is dropped and the cycle begins again.

The game is taut, filled with raw energy. By NHL standards, the play is clean, open and flowing. Women are not allowed to bodycheck at any level. Still, with the stakes so high, it seems inevitable the players will push themselves and their game to the limit and, in the process, test the resolve of the referee.

The Americans are the first to cross the fine line between right and wrong, to catch the ref's eye and succumb to her whistle. They're nailed for two infractions in a row. Then, it's Canada's turn. It starts with Botterill on an iffy call for tripping. Unbeknownst to those of us watching at the time, the Canadian parade to the penalty box has just begun. Before the period is done, three more miscreants, all Canadian, must serve time.

The pattern continues at the start of the second with Kellar for tripping. Stacey Livingstone, the stripe-shirted lady with the red bands on her arms, has become our enemy—and she's an American to boot. Like a card shark at the blackjack table watching his chips slowly dwindle, our emotional reserves are fast depleting as the calls start to mount.

Second Period. The Two-Minute Mark.

Cammi Granato, the American captain, a twelve-year veteran and their most decorated player, is on the ice for every power play. On this, the fifth, she tips a low shot from the point and then her teammate, Katie King, redirects it high over the shoulder of Kim St-Pierre, the Canadian goalie. The score is tied. Canada 1, U.S.A. 1.

"It was inevitable," someone sighs.

Like soldiers to battle, the Canadians forge on.

Second Period. The Four-Minute Mark.

Just inside the U.S. blue line, Campbell spots Danielle Goyette far to her right and feathers a pass to her tape. The wily veteran cuts to the middle and laces a low shot to the net. DeCosta flicks out her left pad, and the puck recoils back to the blue line fast as a snake in the grass. In a burst of raw power, Wickenheiser, the right winger of the veteran trio, barrels toward the rebound. In one fluid motion, she rips a howitzer with laser beam accuracy under the crossbar. DeCosta has no chance. Canada 2, U.S.A. 1.

Our room erupts. "You gotta believe!" someone shouts. Our veterans have showed them.

The penalty total continues to mount. Oullette for roughing, Chartrand for tripping. For every Canadian that's ever laced up the skates, gathered puck and stick and glided across a country pond, or carved figure eights in a cold arena, our team's gritty effort, steely resolve and dogged determination through all the adversity tugs at the heart and roils the gut.

Through it all, Danièle Sauvageau, the Canadian coach, remains as cool as the Utah night air.

"It's not like having a gun to your head," she says afterwards to the scribes who want to know how she felt. An ex-RCMP officer now with the Montreal city police, she, unlike the ones who posed the question, would probably have good reason to know how that feels.

We don't stay quite so cool.

"A load of crap," someone barks when Botterill is fingered again for tripping. "Can you believe it?" another snorts. The penalty count is up to eight in a row.

Second Period. The Last Minute of Play.

Buried deep in our end by the American onslaught, Brisson, thirty-five years of age and a staunch defender, corrals the puck behind the end line. She spots Kellar, the outlet on the left boards. In one well-rehearsed motion, the puck is on Kellar's stick, then on its way down the ice. Like an arrow to the bullseye, the knee-high disc hits Hefford in full flight. A cat on the prowl, she's snuck in behind a pinching American defence and is in alone on the goal. This is the classic one-on-one confrontation: the shooter versus the goalie. Hefford shifts to her right as DeCosta goes down. The shot flutters over the netminder's flailing pad.

Canada 3, U.S.A. 1. There's one second left on the clock.

"The kiss of death," someone exults from the back of the room.

We carry the euphoria into the intermission. A last-minute goal in hockey is the psychological whammy, the hammerlock to the head that every team seeks. Some say it's like scoring two.

The third period begins. Canada continues its march to the box.

Third Period. The Sixteen-Minute Mark

The count is up to thirteen now when the U.S.A. begins another power play. Cammi Granato is on the ice yet again. This time, though, the puck slips across the Canadian blue line to Karyn Bye on the left point. She one-times a shot that skims the ice with eyes for the goal. Kim St-Pierre drops to her knees, a reflex borne out of years of practice, but the puck slips by, just grazing the post.

Canada 3, U.S.A. 2.

The Americans celebrate and head back to centre. Their game has taken on a new life. For four more minutes, we will hang by our fingernails from the edge of the cliff praying for the right ending in this epic battle.

Third Perod. The Last Minute of Play.

Kim St-Pierre is an irresistible force. Three times she tried to make her provincial team with Sauvageau as coach, three times she failed. Still, Sauvageau sensed her talent and brought her to the national level. Now, she's the gatekeeper for her country at the pinnacle of competition. She denies the Americans time after time. When the buzzer sounds, bedlam ensues.

On the ice, St-Pierre is mobbed by her red-crested brigade. They fly at her, bodies piling on bodies. When the frenzy subsides, players untangle and clump in twos and threes chatting, hugging, smiling, some sobbing tears of joy, others tears of relief. Cassie Campbell, the one who told us to forget the losses, stands apart from her mates, the Canadian flag draped over her shoulder, tears welling in her eyes, bottom lip trembling. She looks for all the world like she has nothing left to give, the valve on the pressure cooker finally released.

We stand in the living room, lumps in our throats, waving our own tiny red and white flags. Some of us jump up and down and squeal with delight. "We did it! We did it!" There are hugs and tears and lots of backslapping. We, too, have given all we have to give.

"I knew we could do it," someone asserts conspiratorially.

The victory is ours, the outcome as important to us as to those on the ice. Our egos swell with pride and the joy of accomplishment. Our hockey legacy lives on, its dimensions extended by the girls who just played the game of their lives.

Like all great spectacles, this one, too, has its defining moment. As the celebrations unfold, Danièle Sauvageau, the orchestrator of this epic victory, strides serenely across the ice, seemingly above the fray. She gathers her troops at centre ice. The camera hones in on the tight little circle that's formed around her. Like spokes on a wheel, arms extend into the centre, hands touching in the middle. All eyes focus on their leader.

She speaks these words for the world to hear. "You will go through tough times again in your life. Always, always remember these three words: Responsibility. Determination. Courage. And don't ever give up on you."

For all of us watching this moment unfold, the event has become more than just a gold medal game.

Danièle Sauvageau (centre) and the Canadian women's hockey team celebrate their gold medal victory.   *(CP Picture Archive Mike Ridewood)*

CHAPTER 2
Nagano Tears

"I'm a cop. Cops can't cry."

— Danièle Sauvageau

IN 1988, the Winter Olympics were held in Calgary. For a youthful RCMP officer posted in western Canada and barely a year and a half into her policing career, the buzz of the Games was too strong to resist. Danièle Sauvageau was chosen from her detachment to work in security for the Games' duration. It was a serendipitous selection that over time changed the direction of her life.

"The air was electric with excitement," she recalls. "I remember the events like they were yesterday. Most of the time, I was posted at Calgary Olympic Park where the bobsled, luge and ski jumping took place. Some days, there were 80,000 people at the site, all as excited as me to see Olympians in action. I saw some ice hockey, but the moment of highest drama came when Elizabeth Manley skated to silver [in women's figure skating]. It was so unexpected, and the crowd went wild. When the Olympics ended, I vowed to myself that I would be a part of them one day." She wasn't sure how or when, but she knew her time would come.

In 1994, the International Olympic Committee announced that women's ice hockey would be included in the next Winter Olympics, to be held in Nagano, Japan, in 1998. The promise made by the young police officer in Calgary was about to come true. She would go to her second Olympics, this time as a participant.

After the 1988 Olympics, Sauvageau returned to Montreal and rekindled her passion for coaching. She had become involved as a coach with an elite women's ice hockey team in the city, but quickly worked her way up the ranks, first to the provincial and then to the national levels. The cherry on top of the sundae came when she was appointed assistant coach of the Canadian women's ice hockey team for its inaugural appearance under the five rings of the Olympic movement.

For Sauvageau, the aura of her second Olympics was just as brilliant, just as compelling as her first. Once again, the atmosphere was electric, the event filled with the pomp and ceremony only the Olympics bring. This time, though, there were differences. She was a part of the Canadian contingent, the hit of the party in their oh-so-sporty red Roots jackets and matching berets, marching into the Olympic stadium for the opening ceremonies led by the red Maple Leaf. "I'll never forget stepping into that stadium. It was daylight. There were so many people looking down on us. The ground was white. I felt like I was walking on clouds," she recalls. She stood on the stadium floor surrounded by delegations from more than seventy nations and watched the Olympic flame light the sky and the white balloons signifying peace for the world rise heavenward. She had realized her Olympic dream borne out of Calgary: to return to the Games, not as a spectator but as a participant.

Still, the celebratory mood couldn't lighten the heavy burden these hockey girls bore: the weight of a nation's golden expectations. The Canadians easily defeated Japan, China, Sweden and Finland in the preliminary round before succumbing 7–4 to the U.S.A., now their only threat for Olympic supremacy. Was this a foreshadowing of things to come? Not so, declared a nation steadfast in its belief that the gold medal was Canada's for the taking.

Vicky Sunohara, a Canadian player, remembers the pressure. But for her, there was an added twist. Her grandparents were

Head Coach Shannon Miller (left) and Assistant Coach Danièle Sauvageau behind the bench at the 1998 Olympics in Nagano, Japan.
(CHA Archives)

born fifty miles from Nagano. This Olympic city had wrapped her in its arms like a long-lost child. There was a buzz, like bees to honey, everywhere she went. "We went there with every intention of winning the gold medal," she says. "Every Canadian hockey player really doesn't settle for anything less."

On February 17, 1998, the moment of reckoning arrived. It was the gold medal game. Even when the Americans scored first, the country wasn't deterred. But, somehow, on this day, a Canadian victory was not in the cards. The Americans popped another. The Canadian girls soldiered valiantly on and countered with one. Still, they never seemed to settle. There was an edge to their play that upset their rhythm, a tension and tentativeness that never lifted. In the end, the Americans couldn't be denied, winning 3–1. So often in sport, the examination is taken, then the lesson is given. For the Canadian team, discovering the fine line between wanting to win and being afraid to lose was a tough lesson to learn.

When the final buzzer sounded, the Canadian girls were stunned by the loss. They milled about the ice in dazed silence, chins resting on the taped knobs of their hockey sticks, tears flowing freely. When the American anthem was played and the U.S. flag was raised, the girls looked dreamily into the distance or hung their heads in utter despair.

For Danièle Sauvageau, the assistant coach standing by the crestfallen squad, there was no emotion. "I was just like a block on the ice. There was nothing coming in, nothing coming out, no emotion whatsoever. I felt numb—not mad—just numb. It was unbelievable. I couldn't feel anything. There were people crying all around me and I remember saying to myself, 'I'm a cop. Cops can't cry for the world to see.'"

As the "Star Spangled Banner" played, and the flags went up over the medal ceremony, Danièle made a silent, second Olympic-inspired vow: "I looked at those flags, at the order. It was the U.S.A., Canada, Finland," she states. "I thought to myself, 'That's not right.' Then and there, I vowed I'd be back to change the order, to make it right. It was a dream of mine." The opportunity would come, four years later, to realize her dream.

CHAPTER 3
Beginnings

"You can be anything you want to be."

— Lise Sauvageau

EVEN AS A CHILD, Danièle Sauvageau's mind was always excited by life's possibilities. "Always believe," her parents would tell her. "You can be anything you want to be." When her mother, Lise, asked her at an early age what she wanted to be when she grew up, young Danièle replied with the insight of someone far beyond her years, *"Un sage."* She seemed to understand, even then, the importance of wisdom in life's journey. Her favourite book, discovered at the age of ten, was *Le Petit Prince*, by Antoine Saint-Exupéry, a simple yet profound tale about the meaning of life.

Danièle's journey began in Montreal on April 22, 1962. At the age of four, her insurance-broker father, Marcel, moved the family to Deux-Montagnes, a small town forty kilometres northwest of the city. It was the perfect setting to raise four children. At that time, the place nestled between two mountains was "just like a village," Lise recalls. "You could easily walk to the end of town."

Close by their modest, two-storey house on a street filled with children was the park, a favourite gathering spot for the neighbourhood. Early on, Danièle knew hers was not the bedroom and backyard world of dolls and small talk. The park was the heart of the action, the place for fun and adventure.

Christmas at the Sauvageau home. Left to right: Danièle, Michel (in back), Sylvain, Johanne.
(Sauvageau Family)

The pool and the playground were the big attractions on a hot summer day.

She was a leader even then. Says her mom, "If there was a game of cops and robbers, she was the chief of police, or a game of baseball on the diamond, she organized the teams." There was always a ready assortment of playmates who'd gather in the Sauvageau backyard for a lemonade at the end of their day in the park.

When the sharp bite of winter arrived, life revolved around hockey. Saturday nights, the entire family—including Marcel's brother-in-law, Yvon, and Uncle Germain—would squeeze into the tiny living room and watch their team, the Montreal Canadiens, play hockey on the two-channel TV.

Every Saturday morning, Danièle would escort her two hockey-playing brothers to the local arena. Although a fine little athlete with an overarching desire to excel ("She always had to win the race or be the fastest in the pool," recalls her mom. "It was so important to her to do her best.") Danièle, however, didn't tote a Sherwood and black hockey skates. The girls in Deux-Montagnes did not play organized hockey. In the seventies, hockey was still a boys' preserve in many communities across the country, including Deux-Montagnes. No one gave female players any ice time at the local rinks, and no one pushed hard enough to change the status quo.

It hadn't always been this way for women's hockey. Women in full, ankle-length skirts and turtleneck sweaters were first pictured wearing skates and holding hockey sticks in 1890 on the flooded and frozen lawn of Lord Stanley's vice-regal home, Rideau Hall. Although he was an Englishman who served as the Queen's representative in Canada for only a few years, he loved the game of hockey and invited participants, both male and female, to play on his makeshift ice surface.

Hockey's heyday for women spanned the first three decades of the twentieth century. Practically as many women as men played the game in the twenties and thirties. Hockey was a major sport for women at the University of Toronto, Queen's and McGill. At the club level, the Preston Rivulettes gained national prominence by winning ten Ontario, ten Eastern Canada and six Dominion titles through the thirties. Their record of 348–2 established them, indisputably, as a dynasty in the history of sport, whether male or female.

At the onset of World War II, women's hockey was mothballed for the war effort. When the fighting stopped, men's professional hockey took over the airwaves and the interest of the nation. Ice time at local arenas became the ownership of boys and men.

This dark age in the women's game lasted until the early seventies when females, in ever-growing numbers, began to assert their rights in what had been mostly male domains, and, in hockey, they demanded to play once again. Still, women had to fight to regain a toehold in the sport they loved, to get the ice time and to build their numbers to a level where leagues could be formed. It would take events like the first-sanctioned World Championship in 1990 and, most importantly, the first Olympic participation in 1998, for the women's game to flourish again.

Despite the boom in numbers, even today women's hockey is told to be patient. Sponsors and facilities are hard to get. Women are often at the bottom of the list when it comes to allocating ice time. Female coaches are too rare a breed. In many communities across this nation, there is still no place for women's hockey.

At age ten, in the early seventies, Sauvageau was a girl with a love for the game and no place to play in an organized system, in a small town. In fact, Danièle didn't even own a pair of skates. This, however, didn't stop her from following her brothers out the door every night after dinner. They'd head to the outdoor rink in the park and play shinny until bedtime. Danièle would run up and down the ice in her boots, chasing her brothers for the puck. In her mind, this certainly beat standing on the sidelines watching the boys have all the fun.

The weekend ritual of going to the arena began very early, at 5:00 a.m. This was the only time that ice was available for the young boys. Mr. and Mrs. Sauvageau didn't own a car at the time, so they'd summon a taxi. Ten-year-old Danièle would gather her charges, eight-year-old Michel and five-year-old Sylvain, and off they'd go, through the pitch black of the pre-dawn, still rubbing the sleep from their eyes.

Danièle would lead her brothers to the dressing room, help them don their equipment, get them onto the ice, then act as the gatekeeper at the end of the bench. Even then, the little coach within was coming out. "Play your position, Michel," she'd exhort her talented little brother. "You're all over the ice. Skate hard, Sylvain. You can get that puck." Michel remembers these exhortations fondly. "She was always after

Little Sylvain (No.14) lining up for the face-off at the hockey rink in Deux-Montagnes.   (Sauvageau Family)

us," he recalls, "because she wanted so much to see us do well. She was our coach, and that was that."

These weekly excursions to the rink planted a seed in young Danièle's inquisitive mind. The nuances of the game were unfolding right before her keen and observing eye: a clever give-and-go up the boards, a pinching defenceman joining the rush, a deliberate icing to relieve the pressure. A passion was growing for the game, and an understanding of its intricacies at a level far beyond her years. Subtle as a master scorer's deft touch, a coaching career was taking root.

That the game had truly and forever initiated yet another into its fraternity became evident when Danièle was offered her first real job. The arena manager, needing a reliable teenager to work the snack bar, immediately thought of the energetic and sociable fourteen-year-old, by now a familiar face at the rink. For Danièle, the job came with a necessary perk. "There was a glass partition overlooking the ice," she recalls. "I could flip burgers and sell sodas and watch the game all at the same time. It was my dream job." The vantage point had changed, but the hockey apprenticeship was well on its way.

At the age of sixteen, Danièle enrolled at St. Jerome's College for two years of pre-university study. The school was well over an hour's drive away, which meant leaving home for the first time and living in residence. Her memories of the separation from familiar surroundings are bittersweet ones. "I missed my family terribly, especially my brothers and my older sister Johanne. I would stay at school five days of the week and come home every weekend."

As fate would have it, her new school provided the stage where her embryonic coaching career would officially begin. In her second year of studies, Danièle was walking by the athletic office on her way to class one day. A posting on the notice board caught her eye: "Wanted: Coaches for the boys' and girls' broomball teams. See Monsieur Lauzon if you are interested." Like a cat spotting the mouse, Danièle pounced.

She was an excellent broomball player and knew the game well. In fact, Danièle played every sport going at the time, but because there was no hockey for girls, broomball was a very popular option and the one she focused her energies on. Danièle's club team consistently won the provincial championships and advanced to the nationals. She played defence and, in a game that permitted full body contact, was as tough as an old leather boot. "My opponents would go down the opposite side to the one I was on," she states. "They knew even if the ball got through, they wouldn't."

She rapped on Monsieur Lauzon's door. He listened patiently to her list of attributes. "Okay," he stated and

Danièle, playing
for her college
team at a
provincial broom-
ball tournament,
1982.
(Sauvageau Family)

proposed the obvious. "You can coach the girls' team." Unbeknownst to him, Danièle had a different plan. "Either I coach both the boys' and the girls' teams, or I don't coach at all." For her, it was a point of principle. The man she would be replacing had coached both teams. Why shouldn't she? Monsieur Lauzon was taken aback, but sensed this was a young lady on a mission. It didn't take long for him to agree.

Danièle was only seventeen, the same age as some of her players, but that didn't daunt her. She had her teams, and she relished the challenge. The results were auspicious. She took the boys to the district championship, the winner of which would go to the provincials. She tells the story of the final game. "I looked over at the other bench when the game began.

They had twenty-one players, well over the limit. We lost the game, but not by much. I knew it wasn't fair, so I protested. The committee that reviewed my protest agreed with me. They said I was right, but the result would remain the same. The experience taught me a valuable lesson in life. I found out then you don't always win when you are supposed to. There are injustices." Despite the injustice of this outcome, Danièle's first foray into coaching had tapped into a feeling that would grow, over time, into a passion.

CHAPTER 4

The RCMP

The best of the best.

— RCMP recruiting poster

IN 1971, at age nine, Danièle had an experience that shaped the direction her life would take. She was walking through town on a warm spring day, heading home from school. A police officer, summoned by an emergency call, lay crumpled in a heap at the front door to the local bank. He'd been shot by a would-be robber. The wound wasn't fatal, and the officer recovered, but the attack left a lasting impression on the little girl's mind. "I walked the rest of the way home thinking 'That's not right.' It made me realize I wanted to be someone someday who could change things that just weren't right in the world. Maybe a lawyer, maybe a psychologist, maybe a social worker. I'd always been fascinated by how people behave."

At the end of high school, Danièle headed off to the Université de Montréal, a francophone school in the heart of the downtown where former prime minister Pierre Trudeau once taught law. She embraced her studies in psychology, sociology and management, but by her last year still hadn't decided on a career path.

"The best of the best."

Danièle was walking across campus on a blustery fall day, her mind absorbed by the details of a mid-term paper soon due, when she spotted the headline. It ran in big, bold letters across the top of an RCMP poster hoping to woo civilians to join the force. "Contact your nearest recruitment centre," the poster directed. Danièle turned the idea over. Why not? she thought. Here was a career that incorporated her three most compelling interests: law, psychology and social work. Not long after, she found herself across the desk from a uniformed man.

"You know we only take the best of the best," the recruitment officer announced. His imperious tone suggested she might want to reconsider her interest in the RCMP, but Danièle refused to be intimidated. "I want to apply," she stated matter-of-factly. The man had met his match. The interview continued. He proceeded to explain the application process, which included a physical, psychological and written assessment.

Her family did not know there was an aspiring red-coated Mountie in its midst until an investigator rapped at the front door one evening. He'd come to do a background check on the candidate's character and history, a routine part of the application process. Danièle's father was in the kitchen washing dishes at the time. His only comment to her after the visit: "Is this what you really want to do?"

In the mid-eighties, a successful RCMP candidate was sworn in as a constable first, and then sent to Regina, Saskatchewan, for training. This is the route Daniéle followed.

The Depot, as the training academy is called, is a collection of buildings on the outskirts of Regina near the airport. In the eighties, recruits were subjected to six months of rigorous, paramilitary training. If successful, and not all were, they were awarded the badge of the Royal Canadian Mounted Police.

Danièle arrived at The Depot late on a Friday afternoon in the summer of 1985 to begin her training. "I was handed a pillow, a grey blanket and a set of sheets and escorted to the dormitory. Inside, there were thirty-two beds, sixteen lining one wall, and sixteen along the opposite. Beds were assigned alphabetically. Each sleeping area included a bed and a foldout desk with a lamp. I was told I would be purchasing a trunk to store my clothes. This would be my home for the next six and a half months. At the age of twenty-three, looking around these Spartan quarters, I thought a half a year seemed like an eternity. 'What am I doing here?' I wondered."

The rest of the weekend was set aside for orientation to the new surroundings, a chance to unravel some of The Depot's mysteries, like the location of the swimming pool, the mess hall, the courthouse and the shooting range, and, on the Sunday afternoon, to receive a lesson on bed making, RCMP-style. At 6:00 a.m. on Monday, Danièle and the thirty-one other females assigned to her dorm ran to the parade square to begin their new life together as a troop dedicated to becoming Royal Canadian Mounted Police. At the time, troops were segregated by sex, all male or all female. That practice changed at the end of the eighties.

That Monday evening, ten troops of finely tuned veterans of Depot living performed in the Sunset Parade, a marching show for the newly arrived recruits. They were an impressive sight in their scarlet uniforms and lockstep precision. Inspired by the artistry and athleticism, Danièle vowed then and there she would rise to meet every challenge thrown her way.

A typical day began with reveille at 6:00 a.m., inspection at bedside at 6:30, then an inspection parade in the drill hall. Breakfast followed from 6:45 to 7:30. Beginning at 8:00, the activities for the day were scheduled: classes in enforcement-related topics like law and police practices, human relations and domestic disputes, and practical courses in firearms, swimming, lifesaving, first aid, P.T. (physical training, paramilitary style), self-defence and motor vehicle driving. Foot drill, or marching, was part of daily life as regular as breathing; likewise, the sergeant major's parade occurred every day at noon, rain or shine, on the parade ground; 4:30 to 6:00 p.m. was suppertime. From 6:00 on, Danièle and her troopmates were polishing boots, organizing their kit, cleaning firearms, studying, practising self-defence or running a part of their weekly ten-kilometre quota.

For the first three months of training, running was the norm for all troops. Danièle's troop was no exception. Its members wore the uniform of the unschooled foot soldier: blue runners with the word Canada stitched on the outside of each shoe, brown pants and beige shirt. Ninety days of foot drill passed before they were issued the RCMP uniform, the universally identifiable one with the yellow stripe running the length of each pant leg and the black Mountie boots. The footwear, especially, marked a coming of age in the troop's time together. "These were the boots we'd been polishing for three months but never could wear," Danièle explains. "Now we were good enough to walk as a troop. For the first few days after the issue, I was paranoid about my boots. At meals, I'd tuck my feet under my chair in the dining hall. I didn't want anyone accidentally scuffing my shoes."

Stepping out of line, like wearing boots that didn't shine like black satin, could be costly. The transgressor might find herself on the grounds polishing a life-size replica of a plane made out of steel or, on hands and knees with a toothbrush in tow, cleaning the cracks between the ceramic tiles lining the pool. Danièle was willing to play by the rules of the training game. "Early on, I made a decision: I'll fit in because I don't want to fall out. At The Depot, you learned to accept certain things because that is just the way they are. Our training taught us an important lesson: Put your energy into what you can control."

Throughout the training, the recruits would work on real-life scenarios using volunteers from the town to play the roles. Initially, the scenarios were simple in nature, like responding to a call about a stolen bicycle. But, as the training progressed, the scenarios reflected the diversity of skills needed to do the job. Domestic disputes, robberies and even murders were enacted.

Favourite scenarios for Danièle were those that involved mock trials. "I loved going to the courthouse. It was the idea of having a case, developing a plan, working your way through the investigation, putting the pieces of the puzzle together and presenting your work. Either The Depot instructors or lawyers from town would conduct the trials, putting you on the stand and questioning you on the work you'd done. I enjoyed that challenge."

A half year of intense daily activities and dormitory living with thirty-one troop mates, all of whom were complete strangers in the beginning, fostered intense esprit de corps. The Depot training was all about teamwork, the stronger helping the weaker and, in some cases, the weak not surviving. In Danièle's troop, four bowed out along the way.

The training was also about attention to detail. When the overseeing officer inspected your area, he expected to see clothes hanging in perfect order, shirts buttoned down, shoes polished, the sheets on your cot ten centimetres, no more and no less, from the end of the bed. If you neglected the smallest details, your troopmates suffered. You learned to work as part of a team.

Finally, The Depot training was about evaluation. Progress and performance were measured on an ongoing basis, every day. There were benchmarks to meet in every activity, from physical skills, like running a mile to meet a time, to learning the ABCs of detective work. "If it was about fingerprinting, for example, the challenge initially would be to get a fingerprint off a glass," explains Danièle. "Once that benchmark was met, the next was set. Eventually, the challenge became to find a fingerprint in a house where a crime was committed. Where do you start? The troop would work as a team to achieve these benchmarks."

After six months, Danièle marched with her troopmates in the Pass Out ceremony. She was presented with her badge signifying her status as an officer in the Royal Canadian Mounted Police. For Danièle, it was a moment steeped in pride. "I worked so hard for this badge," she recalls. "Every day, we were challenged, physically and mentally. I learned so much about myself. When they give you your badge, it's like getting a gift. The RCMP is so much a part of our folklore and our culture. I was so proud to be a part of one of the best police departments in the world." When Danièle left The Depot, she took the legacy of her training out into the world to carry with her forever.

Danièle's troop marches in formation for the last passage, a part of the RCMP graduation ceremony at The Depot.
(Sauvageau Family)

Danièle receives her RCMP badge in the drill hall at The Depot.
(Sauvageau Family)

25

Danièle pictured in her RCMP uniform with her badge in hand. She made it! (Sauvageau Family)

CHAPTER 5
Powell River

Seeds of doubt.

ONCE GRADUATED from The Depot, constables are assigned to a detachment. They are not guaranteed a placement in their area of choice and could find themselves located to a posting in Inuvik, Northwest Territories, bordering the Arctic Ocean, in Goose Bay, Labrador, overlooking the Atlantic or in one of hundreds of places in between. British Columbia, a province without a provincial police force, unlike Ontario, Quebec or Newfoundland, boasts the highest number of RCMP detachments and officers in the country. Danièle Sauvageau, with her posting to Powell River, joined the B.C. ranks, separating her approximately 3,000 kilometres from her home in Deux-Montagnes, Quebec. The bigger separation, however, was ultimately the gulf created between her family, language and culture and her new home.

A person would be hard-pressed to find a more idyllic setting than Powell River, known to many as the hidden treasure. Located on the Upper Sunshine Coast of British Columbia, across the Georgia Strait from Vancouver Island, the town sits at the mouth of a long fjord cutting deeply into the Coast Mountain Range of the Rockies. Its backdrop is as stunning as an Emily Carr canvas: rolling hills, forested slopes and peaks adorned with shimmering white glaciers. The place has long been a mecca for outdoor enthusiasts, with the mountains, the elongated Powell Lake and the sea a playground for hikers, sailors, anglers and year-round golfers.

Originally established as a mill town in 1910, the small city of 23,000 now includes a thriving artistic community. Tourists flock to their hideaways in the summer even though the only access is by sea or air. It's an hour and a half ride by ferry across the strait from Vancouver Island, or a four-hour, two-ferry ride from Vancouver, 142 kilometres to the south, with a one and a half hour drive up the Sechelt Peninsula to end the journey.

Danièle arrived at her posting late in the evening and was received by the sergeant on duty. "Where should I stay?" asked the newcomer to town. The officer named a hotel, one of three to choose from. "You know you have two strikes against you," he began, then paused for effect before continuing. "You're French and you're female." Danièle later discovered he was three weeks from retirement; a woman working in the world of policing, and a French one at that, was not a notion he could easily accept. Danièle headed out of the office into the night. "What am I doing here?" she wondered once again.

Twenty-four RCMP officers are assigned to the Powell River Detachment. The town itself is only one small part of their jurisdiction, which follows the indented coastline fifty kilometres from Saltery Bay in the south to Lund in the north. The area also includes two islands just off the coast, Texada and Savary.

Despite her less than friendly welcome, Danièle soon settled in. Life as an RCMP officer in this small, semi-isolated community was friendly and laid back. She rented a house from Dennis Oliver, a paper mill worker in town. It had a view over the ocean and an eagle's nest in a tree at the end of the street. Dennis quickly became a father figure, happy to show Danièle nature's delights on the West Coast from his four-seater Cessna. "I remember looking down at the most awesome vistas of rugged mountain tops, snaking glaciers and

Danièle is ready to begin her first day of work in Powell River, B.C.
(Danièle Sauvageau)

azure seas. I'd never seen such rugged wild beauty in my life. Sometimes, a group of us would go to the lake, catch some trout and have a fresh fish fry for dinner. It was a totally different world for me."

For someone wearing the badge for the first time, Powell River was as gentle an introduction to policing as any place could be. "We had the routine duties to do, like answering calls about wandering dogs and breaking up fights in the bar.

29

Danièle and Dennis Oliver stand in front of his Cessna.   (Danièle Sauvageau)

Sometimes, the toughest part was finding my way through town to get to the problem," Danièle recalls. She was on her own now: one person, one car. "I had a trainer, Len Lasseur, one of the officers in the detachment. He was the one I could call if I needed help. When you're by yourself, twenty-three years old and running after someone heading into the bush after a break-in, well, it's a little intimidating.

"Language was a problem, too. I remember a colleague telling me I'd be working the graveyard shift. I had no idea what that was."

Like any detachment across the country, there were aspects of the job that made the place unique. Clam digging, for Danièle, surely counted as one. "I'll never forget my first inspection of a clam digging site," she begins. "Myself and another officer left the detachment in the wee small hours of the morning. It was a fifteen-minute boat ride to Savary Island, a beautiful, forested tract edged by kilometres of golden-sand beach. At the time, I had no idea the place was a clam digger's paradise. For a city girl from Montreal, I hadn't a clue what clam digging was about. I didn't know that when the tide goes out, the commercial operators move in, pulling the clams from the wet sand. It's a big industry on this part of the West Coast. So there I stood, at four in the morning among the harvesters and their buckets, making sure no one surpassed his quota."

In the end, it wasn't the clam digging or the munitions checks on the lumbering faction, Powell River's economic mainstay, that made Danièle rethink her role. The seeds of doubt were planted when she first landed on the West Coast, separated by a chain of mountains and four provinces from her family and her heritage. She had embraced Powell River and the lifestyle, but quickly realized her RCMP career would likely begin and end in British Columbia. "If they had told me I'd be there for fifteen years, I would have stayed. Because I spoke French as well as English, and I was a woman, I was a valuable addition to the force on the West Coast. It became evident to me that I would likely spend my whole career in British Columbia."

In the end, Danièle couldn't reconcile being away from her family for this long. Overriding everything, she wanted the option of seeing her parents grow old.

A year and a half into her posting, Danièle made the most difficult decision of her life. She decided to hand in her badge and go home. Her policing career would move in a different direction. "I had worked so hard to get this badge," she says. "It was like giving back a part of me."

CHAPTER 6

The 1990s

"I am here to lead, not to please."

— Danièle Sauvageau

DANIÈLE'S DECISION to leave the RCMP did not spell the end of her policing career, one to which she was totally committed. Instead, in 1988, she returned to her birthplace, Montreal, and commenced her duties with the Montreal Urban Community Police Service. Here, she was an hour's drive away from her parents' home in Deux-Montagnes and still pursuing the work she loved. The move back East also enabled her to tap into a lingering passion, ice hockey. Through contacts in town, she assumed an administrative position with a top-level local women's hockey club named Ferland 4-Glace.

Her timing was impeccable. At this time, there were approximately 7,000 women hockey players registered in leagues across the country. Not only was there growth at the club level, the game was about to acquire an international presence. Canada had hosted the first invitational world championship in Mississauga, Ontario, in 1987. Three years later, Ottawa hosted the first world championship sanctioned by the International Ice Hockey Federation. Teams from the United States, Sweden, Finland and Canada took part.

Two of the players on Ferland 4-Glace, a thirty-year-old named France St-Louis and a twenty-eight-year-old goaltender,

Denise Caron, were selected to that first national team. Both had watched and played hockey ever since they could remember. In the seventies and eighties, the Montreal Canadiens were still a powerhouse in the National Hockey League. Hockey in Quebec was akin to religion. On Saturday nights in the winter they, like most Quebeckers, cheered for their hockey heroes: Savard, Lafleur, Henri "Pocket Rocket" Richard, Cournoyer and the unflappable Ken Dryden. As youngsters, neither played organized hockey because there were no leagues for girls. They had to feed their desire to play the game they loved in pickup games with their brothers and friends. The circumstances mirrored Sauvageau's. As a ten-year-old, the only outlet for her passion was to stand at the end of the bench cheering her brothers and their teammates on.

Two trailblazers leading the way for young girls in hockey in the late seventies and early eighties were Gail Cummings and Justine Blainey. Gail was an eleven-year-old in 1977 playing goal for a boys' all-star team in Huntsville, Ontario. In the spring of that year, she was barred from the team for the playoffs. Her mother took her case to the Ontario Human Rights Commission. It eventually wound its way through the court system in Ontario, but by the time a ruling came down in her favour, Gail had lost interest in hockey. Justine Blainey's case followed a similar course. In 1985, she elected to play for a boys' peewee team in Etobicoke, Ontario, even though there was a girls' team in the area. The Ontario Human Rights Commission backed Justine's right to play for the boys, but the decision was appealed by the Ontario Hockey Association and the Ontario Women's Hockey Association, who felt Justine should play with the girls. Four years and $150,000 later, the case wound up in the Supreme Court of Canada, which ruled in Justine's favour, decreeing that the ban on girls playing on boys' hockey teams was unconstitutional and discriminatory.

By the time the rulings were passed down, women's hockey was beginning to grow, and more and more women were demanding ice time. A few women's teams had sprouted in the

Montreal area, and St-Louis and Caron found their niche on Ferland 4-Glace. Little did either know at the time that the newly arrived administrator, Danièle Sauvageau, would soon become coach of their club team and that this would be the start of a prominent hockey career for her.

St-Louis tells the story of Danièle's appointment as coach. "One weekend, our club team was playing a tournament in Bromont in the Eastern Townships. Danièle was there in her administrative capacity. Our coach at the time was suspended for arguing with the referee, leaving us without a coach. We looked around and quickly decided Danièle was the most capable of filling his shoes because she had some coaching experience, and she was willing to assume his duties. She became and remained our coach." Thus began a journey that would take Coach Sauvageau to the pinnacle in women's hockey over the next twelve years.

Danièle sensed the possibilities for her in coaching as early as the fall of 1990 when she attended the first World's as a spectator. "I was watching the action with some of my hockey-playing friends," she says. "We were just joking around when I said 'I am going to be national coach one day.'"

Her friends might have taken her comment lightly, but Danièle had steeled her resolve. Soon after the World's, she began the process of becoming a national level coach. She had taken coaching courses in 1987 in Powell River to develop her expertise and soon realized she had entered a male preserve where the attitude toward female interlopers was rigid and, often, unwelcoming. She remembers walking into a room full of men to start her Advanced 1 course for experienced coaches. Many were seasoned veterans, working the bench at the highly competitive midget and junior levels of hockey. "The first man approached me with this comment: 'You must be the team manager.' I replied that, on the contrary, I was a coach, too. An opportunity came on the final day of our course to coach a scrimmage being held that evening at a Midget Triple A tryout camp. I volunteered to coach one of the sides with a colleague. When I returned from lunch that day, the team leader of my coaching group was waiting for me on the steps outside our site. I knew immediately what he was thinking, so I started speaking for him: 'You're going to tell me the parents aren't ready and the players aren't ready for a female coach. Maybe we should rethink tonight's arrangement.' He nodded his head. This was the attitude I had to deal with."

Danièle stayed with Ferland 4-Glace for eight seasons, as well as becoming a part of the coaching staff for the Quebec provincial team. In 1994, Quebec won the ESSO Women's National Championship, the top senior women's event at the highest competitive level. The team repeated the feat over the next two years. St-Louis played on all of those teams. She, for one, didn't doubt Danièle's ability to get to the top. "Knowing her, I could tell she really enjoyed coaching," she said. "When she was head coach on the Quebec team, I could see she wanted to reach the top. When she has an idea," St-Louis pauses, "not much will stop her."

Ferland 4-Glaces compete in the national championship in Ottawa. Danièle, on the far right, holds the Quebec sign.   (Team Album)

35

"People ask me what she is like as a coach," St-Louis adds. "I tell them she is a strong woman. She is not afraid to stand up and lead. You have to have that talent, that ability, if you want to be head coach. She would often remind the players 'I am here to lead, not to please.'"

A momentous event for women's ice hockey occurred in 1994 when the International Olympic Committee announced that the event would be included for the first time at the Olympics at the 1998 games in Nagano, Japan. For Sauvageau, the announcement fired her imagination and added more fuel to her burning desire to coach. "I immediately knew that I wanted to be part of the Olympic experience. I really got involved doing scouting and evaluation." She continued taking courses in coaching, working toward a master's level, and learning as much about the game as she could.

With her success at the provincial level, it wasn't long before Danièle was turning heads on the national front. Her name was added to a select list of coaches earmarked by the CHA as national calibre. The roster included Shannon Miller, Melody Davidson, Julie Healy and Karen Hughes. Danièle's selection as assistant coach of the Canadian team for the 1995 Pacific Rim Tournament in San Jose, California, marked her first international experience at the senior level. Canada won gold against teams from the United States, Japan and China. In 1996, Danièle received her first national level appointment as head coach. She led the under nineteens at a tournament in Lake Placid against the United States. Her assistant was Karen Hughes, an up-and-comer from Ontario. Their paths were destined to cross again three years later.

The upward curve continued: assistant coach of the gold medal winners at the inaugural 1996 Three Nations Cup in Ottawa against Finland and the United States;[1] assistant coach

---

[1]This tournament was introduced to provide more competition at the highest level in women's hockey. Eventually, Sweden was added to the mix and the event was dubbed the Four Nations Cup.

of the gold medal team at the 1997 World Championship in Kitchener, Ontario;[2] assistant coach of the silver medal team at the 1997 Three Nations Cup in Lake Placid, New York; and, finally, an ambition realized, assistant coach of the Canadian team heading to Nagano, Japan, for the 1998 Olympics. Danièle's Olympic-inspired vow in 1988 to return to the Games as a participant one day had become a reality. "This is a dream come true for me," she said. "Hockey is my passion and coaching is my avenue to express that passion. I will do whatever it takes to get the job done."

Six months prior to the Games, the Canadian team centralized in Calgary to prepare. Sauvageau had been in Calgary since the fall of 1996 working at the newly established Women's High Performance Centre for ice hockey at the Calgary Oval and preparing for the World's in '97. For her, it was an opportunity to immerse herself in hockey at the highest level. For the most part of eight years since her return to Montreal, she'd combined hockey and policing. Throughout those years, she'd worked long hours to accommodate both. In Calgary, she could concentrate solely on hockey for the first time in her life.

When the drive to the Olympics began with centralization, the pace accelerated once again. Sauvageau reflects on the experience. "In a way, we were guinea pigs. This was the first time for the national team to come together over an extended time frame. Perhaps, as coaches, we were a little too ambitious. In six months, there was no time off. I think the notion was 'the more we give the players, the better they're going to get.' In the end, the team was probably overtrained." Danièle's duties included goaltending, the penalty kill, scheduling and team building.

---

[2]The event was given extensive media coverage and was played in front of packed arenas. This, along with the high-profile women's hockey received at Nagano, sparked a boom in the number of girls and women playing hockey in Canada.

Shannon Miller, the first full-time coach with the national team, ran the show. She began her hockey career as a player, appearing in the first-ever women's national championship in 1982. Throughout the eighties and early nineties she worked tirelessly to build the hockey programs in Saskatchewan and Alberta. Her first national appointment came in 1992 as the assistant coach for the Canadian entry at the World's in Finland. Her résumé grew quickly as the appointments mounted. She assumed the head coach's mantle in 1995 and never looked back. Passionate about hockey, she started the first women's high-performance program in ice hockey at the Olympic Oval and brought Sauvageau on board to help run it. The program at the Oval offered elite players from across the country a place to train intensely with excellent facilities and under the watchful eyes of the sport science staff. When Miller left her position with the national team after Nagano, she headed south to the States and built another topnotch women's ice hockey team at the University of Minnesota in Duluth. Under her guidance, the team quicky garnered two National Collegiate Athletic Association titles.

Like Sauvageau, Miller had a policing background, working as an officer in the Calgary police force. This career was on hold while the team prepared for Nagano.

Miller had a long-standing reputation as a tough taskmaster. Asked how far she would go to guarantee a victory in Nagano, Miller stated that she'd work her team twenty hours a day if that's what it took.

Ray Bennett, a thirty-four-year-old from Red Deer, Alberta, rounded out the coaching triumvirate. He had worked primarily at junior- and college-level hockey on the men's side, coming on board with the women's team at the World's in Kitchener in 1997. He believed strongly in his charges. "I think these girls understand the game and play it at a level relative to other women's national teams like no other team in the world." His unbounded optimism was well grounded. The only blemish for the Canadian side on an otherwise impeccable record since women's hockey arrived on the world stage in 1990 was a silver-medal performance at the Three Nations Cup in Lake Placid. A country with hockey bred in its bones could reasonably expect Olympic gold from these girls.

From the moment the team landed on Japanese soil, the players knew all of their sacrifices over the years were worth it. For St-Louis, now one of the Olympians, Nagano was her best experience as an athlete. "In hockey, when we went to tournaments, we would just meet other hockey players. Here, we met all the great athletes in all the other sports from all over the world. We met the Japanese people and experienced their culture. Everything was provided for us. Their generosity of spirit was unparalleled."

The Nagano setting with its mountain backdrop was striking enough to uplift the most apprehensive spirit. Sauvageau came to the Olympics filled with hope. The first dark cloud, however, appeared on her horizon when Team Canada tied Sweden 1–1 in an exhibition game. Since 1990 and the onset of international competition, Canada had dominated the Swedes in every match the two teams had played. Sauvageau started to wonder about the team's preparation with this result. Her concern grew when the U.S.A. skated over the Canadians 7–4 in the preliminaries.

On the bus ride to Big Hat arena for the gold-medal game, the team was as tight as an elastic band stretched to its limit. Sauvageau describes the atmosphere: "The bus was so quiet. It was like a morgue. Everyone was very tense. I wondered 'What's going to happen?' I was questioning whether we had done everything we needed to do. Maybe our focus was too narrow. We'd lost sight of the big picture, what the Olympics were really about in our quest for gold. Then, in a flash, the game was over. The Americans had beaten us three to one. We didn't win gold. Our Olympic dream was shattered."

Sauvageau talks about the weight of expectations: "We didn't really peak at the right time. There was a lot of pressure on us. We didn't want to admit it. Everybody expected us to win the gold medal, and I think we drowned under the pressure. It was the first experience for everyone—the coaches, the players, the administrative staff. In Nagano, there were a lot of adjustments to make: odd training times, an unpredictable transportation system, tight living quarters, a mindset that needed to keep everything in perspective. The Americans had been together since 1996. We had five months to prepare. In the end, it was not enough time."

Even if there were tough lessons to be learned from Nagano, Danièle recognized it as a turning point for the sport. "It put women's hockey on the map. People who never watched hockey before became interested in the sport. Sponsors came on board. The number of girls and women playing the game jumped dramatically from around seven thousand in 1990 to close to sixty thousand by the end of 1998. That's what the Olympics did."

Still, the loss gnawed at Sauvageau. She was eager for redemption. Danièle was presented with her opportunity on June 15, 1998, when the CHA, after a series of interviews with a number of candidates, elevated Sauvageau to the position of head coach. For the first time, she was truly in the driver's seat. Once again, she'd be working with Karen Hughes, her colleague with the under nineteens in 1996.

Hughes had worked as head coach at her alma mater, the University of Toronto, since 1993. As a student at the university, she'd obtained her undergraduate degree in commerce and completed her master's in community and neighbourhood planning. Coaching was strictly a part-time vocation. Like all the women coaching at the national level, this lined her pockets with nickels and dimes. To earn a living meant working full-time outside hockey. Her other job was with the Ontario government as a senior advisor to the Ontario Provincial Management Board Secretariat.

Joining Sauvageau and Hughes was Ken Dufton, a rookie on the national scene but a man who'd garnered an impressive record with the Beatrice Aeros, an elite senior club team in

Ontario that was a spawning ground for numerous national players over the years. Dufton had finished his playing career in his teens, at the triple A, or highest level of midget hockey. His coaching career began at the tender age of eighteen with a boys' team. He'd never considered women's hockey until a friend asked him to help out at a few practices. "I couldn't believe the difference. The girls actually came over to me to say 'thank you' at the end of practice. That was it for me. I started coaching the Aeros and never looked back."

His career as a head coach with the Aeros had spanned nearly twenty years. His invitation to join the national team came with a revised job description. "As a head coach, I knew what I wanted from my assistants, and I was determined to give the same to Danièle." If he was apprehensive about working under a woman, his concerns soon vanished. "She made it easy. Whether or not it's her policing background, I don't know, but she is the kind of person who wants information, the more the better. I never doubted I'd be asked my opinion. Some assistants get panicky because they don't think they will have a say. I was always given the opportunity to share my information. Danièle had the final say in the decision-making, but she never made her decision without my and Karen's input."

For the coaching team, the challenge was clear from the outset: to somehow cure the "Nagano Hangover." Danièle was adamant. "So many people ask, 'Why?' It's time to move on from there." Like St-Exupéry in *Le Petit Prince*, she found wisdom in a young child, her five-year-old niece, Melissa. "When she talks about events in her life, whether they happened a day, a week or a month ago, she says, 'That was yesterday.' In other words, it's over, so just move forward."

Since the end of the Nagano Games, Danièle had never stopped thinking, planning, reflecting on a new course of action. The year leading up to Nagano had been an emotional one. The time had come to shift the focus to a more businesslike approach. In her mind, the plan would be a long-term one, a four-year process leading to Salt Lake City.

The first Olympics had been a learning experience for everyone. For two weeks, the team had been under the microscope, viewed by the eyes of the world. This kind of scrutiny exacted a toll. Somehow, Danièle knew, the team had to learn to cope. "Stress can be a positive force," she mused, "but if you become afraid to lose, it takes away from your ability to perform. The hockey stick becomes a four-by-four in your hands and the hockey puck, a golf ball."

The first order of business in her new position was to implement an effective evaluation system. "So often," says Danièle, "players compare themselves to each other. We wanted to shift that focus. Every player brings different strengths to the ice." The upcoming season would include a Three Nations Cup and a world championship in Finland.

In October 1998, an evaluation camp was held to select a team for the Three Nations Cup. Forty-five players were invited to Calgary. Every player who attended the camp left with a written evaluation of her performance to take back to her club coach. The assessment included the player's three strengths, three areas for improvement and a comment on her mental approach and consistency. The coaching staff wanted the cards laid on the table for all to see. This kind of transparency was a first in hockey at the national level. Over the long haul, Danièle was confident that this kind of feedback with clearly communicated expectations for each player would ensure that coaches and players were on the same page. It would also mean that the onus of responsibility and accountability for training and development rested squarely on the players' broad shoulders where, Sauvageau's career experience and instincts told her, it belonged.

A second key cog in the performance wheel was to have each player understand her role on the team. Dufton, for one, respected the new head coach's honest approach in telling her players where they stood. "Take St-Louis," he says. "She was thirty-nine at the time. It's never easy telling a player she is nearing the end of the road. In the summer of 1998, she met with Danièle. St-Louis asked outright, 'Do I have a chance to make this team?' Danièle was forthright. She told her there were four people vying for the fourth line centre. Was she prepared to sacrifice everything for a shot at that? This wasn't the role St. Louis was accustomed to playing. She'd been a first and second line pivot throughout her career. Nevertheless, she decided to try. I respect Danièle for being so honest. I think it is important to give players feedback, not only on their skills but on their roles on the team."

In December, twenty players travelled to Finland for the Three Nations Cup. The lineup included a smattering of rookies getting their first chance with the big team; the rest were veterans who were holdovers from the Olympics. Danièle describes the setting: "Here we were at a training centre five hours north of Helsinki very close to the Arctic Circle. It was December. There must have been three hours of daylight. I don't even call it light. I call it grey. It was such a different environment for us." Danièle and her coaching team had worked hard in the months leading up to the cup to erase the dark shadow of Nagano.

The championship game was against the U.S.A. Canada won 4–3 in a shoot-out. For the Nagano veterans, lining up on the blue line to hear the Canadian anthem once again was the big first step on the road to redemption.

The World's were held back in Epsoo, Finland, a suburb of Helsinki, in April 1999. There were nine new players on the team this time. Looking down the road to Salt Lake City, Danièle had deemed it critical to give raw talent the chance to make its mark with the big team.

Sami Jo Small and Kim St-Pierre, two young backstoppers, were brought on board for the long haul. In another key move, Cassie Campbell was shifted from the blue line up to forward. Sauvageau reasoned that her defensive skills upfront would serve the team well on the penalty kill. St-Louis, with a decade of international experience under her belt, had one last chance to leave her game at the top.

A veteran squad laced with youthful exuberance proved a potent mix. The youngsters brought with them the outlook and attitude of the little engine that could. Like the red locomotive that surmounted every obstacle in its path, the team chugged to victory, defeating its arch rival, the U.S.A., 3–1 in the final. Another notch, the fifth in a row, was carved in Team Canada's world championship belt.

Sauvageau had allotted St-Louis a regular shift as a fourth line centre, which only made the player's taste of victory that much sweeter. The aging star could happily retire with gold medal in hand. The ghost of Nagano had been exorcised.

Sauvageau's first year at the helm of the national team had been a success. The national team had turned a corner. Nagano was yesterday. The road ahead was a straight one, all the way to Salt Lake City. Little did Sauvageau know at the time, however, there would be an unexpected detour along the way.

CHAPTER 7

The Montreal Rocket

"A man or a woman, how important is that? When you know what you're doing, it doesn't matter."

— Gaston Therrien, head coach, Montreal Rocket

ON APRIL 9, 1999, Tom Renney, CHA vice-president, informed Danièle that her one-year contract to coach the national team was not being renewed. Instead, Melody Davidson, head coach of the national under twenty-two team was being promoted to lead the big team into the 2000 season. According to Mr. Renney, the reasons were simple and easy to understand: the organization knew what Danièle could do; the time was ripe to give someone else a chance. "It is incumbent upon us to make the female game strong, and that means seeing that there are more people capable of doing the job," he stated publicly at the time. The decision was made despite Sauvageau's 14–1–0 record for the 1999 season, including gold medals at both the Three Nations Cup and the World's.

When the formal announcement was made, the press and the public were aghast at the seeming injustice of the move. They quickly lined up in Danièle's corner. Jim Taylor of the *Calgary Sun* wrote in his column that Scotty Bowman's record of consecutive Stanley Cup wins would never have happened if the Detroit Red Wings had thought this way. He suggested sarcastically that perhaps the tie had been Danièle's undoing. Dave Stubbs, a sportswriter for the *Montreal Gazette* was bemused by the notion the CHA put forward that it was "not demoting Sauvageau, but rather helping her to expand her horizons." Guy Blondeau, CEO of Hockey Quebec, spoke for himself and his province when he said, "We are shocked and saddened by this decision. We don't understand it." France St-Louis, freshly retired and no longer needing to worry about who was issuing the orders from behind the bench, felt the CHA had delivered a low blow. "Danièle worked under tremendous pressure after Nagano. We won everything, and now the CHA won't give her a guarantee, or even a hint about her future," she stated.

Karen Hughes, her assistant for the 1999 season, describes how she found out. "Our season ended with the world championships on March 14. Danièle had flown from Montreal to Calgary on Friday, April 9, for the CHA year-end meetings. Ken Dufton and I left on the Saturday morning from Toronto. We met Danièle at the airport in Calgary. She looked shaken, and then she said, 'They are not having me back.' There was a moment of stunned silence. Ken and I were shocked and upset. We couldn't have had a more successful season. We had meetings scheduled for the rest of the day at the CHA offices. Needless to say, it was very uncomfortable for everyone involved. I remember it being a very long day."

Danièle was stunned and hurt by the decision. She'd worked long and hard to get to the top and had proven her merit with her unblemished record. What more could the CHA want? Despite her disappointment, she remained true to form, unwilling to throw stones willy-nilly at anybody. She bore no malice toward her replacement, Melody Davidson, one of eleven people short-listed for the job. "Mel had nothing to do with the hiring. She simply threw her hat in the ring like the rest of us." At her most emphatic, she suggested that if the powers-that-be at the CHA thought she'd just sit around for a year waiting for their next appointment, well, they were mistaken. In her mind, one thing was certain. She would not play the role of a victim. The CHA had stated that Danièle would still have responsibilities with the national team related to scouting and evaluation. However, she was about to embark on a different journey.

Upon returning to Montreal, Danièle began scouting the possibilities. The Quebec Major Junior League, one of three national major junior loops in the country supplying the NHL with talent via the entry draft, had just announced the addition of a new team to the league, the Montreal Rocket. The mecca of hockey had not harboured a major junior franchise since the 1981–82 season. Major junior teams were sprinkled throughout the province in places like Laval, Sherbrooke, Rimouski, Granby, Val-d'Or and Chicoutimi, where life in the town, when the first snow fell, revolved around hockey for a sizeable core.

Montreal was a big city with lots of activities to pull people away from the junior game. Two decades previously, the crowds weren't there, and the juniors left town. In 1999, a group of business people were ready to try again, this time with the Rocket.

Ever the visionary and pioneering spirit, Danièle was struck by an idea: why not coach major junior? Hockey at this level was truly a male domain. No woman's presence had ever graced the bench of a major junior team. Like a carrot dangled in front of a hungry rabbit, the idea drew Danièle on. In the end, the challenge was too much to resist.

She approached Gaston Therrien, the Rocket's newly appointed head coach. Gaston agreed to set up an interview. He remembers the vow he made to his wife and himself at the time. "I told my wife the night before our meeting, 'If this woman looks me straight in the eye when I ask her a question, I will hire her.'"

The next day at the interview, Therrien cut straight to the chase. "You know, Danièle, this won't be easy. You are dealing with sixteen- to twenty-year-old boys. Don't forget, they are not adults; they are still boys. They can be difficult at times. You are a woman, and the first one. They will test you. Are you ready for this?" Danièle looked her interrogator straight in the eye. "No trouble at all," she replied. "I am a cop. I'm used to working with all kinds of people. I think I can handle these young men."

Therrien, true to his word, hired the first female coach ever at this level. To him, her talent was abundantly clear. "A man or a woman, how important is that? When you know what you're doing it doesn't matter."

Danièle is the cover girl for the Montreal Rocket.   (Team Archives)

Because Danièle was, once again, working full time for the Montreal Urban Community Police Service, it was agreed that she would attend practices and home games only. She would not be expected to travel with the team. Gaston and his assistant, Gilbert Delorme, would work the bench. Danièle would be the third pair of eyes, seated in the stands with a bird's eye view of the on-ice action. She'd monitor the play, and share her observations as the game unfolded. There was one adjustment she had to make. The young men she watched were strong and quick. Their play was faster than the women's game, and she had to think and assess very quickly. Although difficult at first, the experience honed to a razor's edge an already sharp eye for the game.

Her analytical mind and technical expertise were a perfect fit for the task at hand. The women's game relied on systems, finesse and teamwork. Its intricacies were hot-wired into her brain. In many ways, it was more complicated than the junior game where the deck was stacked for speed and power. The boys realized early on that this was a woman who knew her hockey. Louis Robitaille, a first-year player, remembers her first day on the job. "When I arrived at the Montreal camp, I was new to the league. Here was this woman, brand new, too, among all the guys. Someone told me she was an assistant coach. At first I was doubtful, but she was such a calm person. If she was wowed by the guys, she sure didn't show it. I don't think she changed her coaching style at all for us."

For Danièle, that first day was one to remember, too. "Because I was the first woman to coach major junior, when I walked into that camp, I knew everybody was watching me: the way I was walking, the way I was talking, the way I was smiling. There were so many eyes looking at me, I began to wonder if I could even skate."

It didn't take long for Coach Sauvageau to earn the respect of her charges. She prowled the ice or stood by the boards watching, listening, always learning. When an opportunity surfaced, she'd don her teaching hat and deliver a lesson.

Young Robitaille was impressed. "She was never a cheerleader, clapping her hands like some assistants do. She didn't say much, but when she spoke you listened. She explained things so well. If someone was talking while she was speaking, her voice would change and she'd look at us differently. She soon let us know we all had to be on the same channel."

"I believe I made them feel good about themselves," Danièle explains. "In men's hockey, so much comes down to 'You're not good' or 'You're good.' I tried to tell the players the whys and the hows, the whats to do, instead of the what nots. I wanted to give them information so they could become better hockey players."

Before every game and between periods, Danièle talked about strategy with her colleagues. Sometimes, she'd enter the dressing room and tell the boys directly what she was seeing on the ice. "Ask her anything about hockey—the power play, the penalty kill—it doesn't matter. She has the answers," Robitaille declares.

As the season progressed, Danièle worked just as diligently on the mental side of the game. Says Robitaille, "She's never beat before a game. No matter how good the other team looked, and we were far from the best team in the league, there was never a game Danièle went into thinking she wouldn't win. She refused to let us quit. I don't know how many times she came into the dressing room and said, 'Come on guys, you're not dead yet.'"

Danièle was eager to step behind the bench. The opportunity came when Delorme, behind the bench with Therrien, was called out of town before a home game. Gaston brought Danièle down from the stands to work with him alongside the boys. She knew she was back where she belonged. She stayed behind the bench for the rest of the year providing individual feedback to the players and to Gaston.

The Rocket's seventy-two-game season ended with a 29–32–6 record, not unexpected for a team new to a league where the play is fast and the opposition unforgiving. For

Danièle, the season was a winning one. Team Canada's victory at the World's in Finland in April 1999 with Sauvageau at the helm and her work with the Rocket had impressed her peers in the coaching community. The Coaching Association of Canada voted her Coach of the Year for the 1999–2000 season and Sport Québec voted her Coach of the Year in Quebec. The public acclaim was just the icing on the cake. She had relished the opportunity to go to the rink every day, to be on the ice with the players challenging her to come up with new drills on a daily basis, and to work with the team in innovative ways. More importantly, the experience would stand her in good stead for the as yet unknown challenges that lay ahead.

CHAPTER 8

Juggling Two Careers

"Hockey is only a game."

— Danièle Sauvageau

THE Montreal Urban Community Police Service started patrolling the streets of Montreal in 1972 when police services covering twenty-nine municipalities in and around the island of Montreal were amalgamated into one of the largest forces in Canada. Today, the force is more than 4,400 officers strong.

In 1989, Danièle enlisted with the service. Living out west since 1986, her return to Montreal was a homecoming of sorts. She was born here. She had lived here until she was four, playing on its streets and in its parks. She spent her university years here. She knew the city well and loved its ambience.

She smiles at the memory of her first day on the job. "They said, 'The keys are in the cruiser. You're an ex-RCMP officer, you'll have no problem finding your way.'" The reality was she didn't know the part of the city patrolled by her division, with its labyrinthine streets and back alleys.

Sharing the front seat of the patrol car was a fresh-faced rookie named Marc Tanguay. Danièle would be his mentor for the first nine months of his policing career. She left a big impression on him. "She gave me confidence. She was such a great leader. We had so much fun together," he says.

"I remember one incident of a fire," Tanguay continues, "in a large residential building complex on Pierrefonds Boulevard.

We were on our way to the station for lunch and noticed the smoke from the street, just as the fire trucks were arriving. Without hesitation, we went into the burning building to evacuate some of the residents from some of the ninety apartment units. We were inside without any breathing equipment in smoke-filled corridors directing and carrying people downstairs. We even became overcome by the smoke and had to make our way to a balcony to be rescued by the firemen.

"Besides the smoke we were fine, but for our troubles we were told that it was not our job to go into burning buildings . . . that our job was to direct traffic on the outside perimeter. I know to this day that we saved lives that day because the firemen didn't start coming into the building 'til we had evacuated almost everyone. . . . I'm pretty sure that had I been with someone else that day that we would never have gone into that building. Regardless of what people said or thought, regardless of the little recognition we received, I think we did the right thing. That day she taught me what the real meaning of policing was—to help others at a time when they are most in need, and to be a constant professional."

The job of the cop on the street is to respond to emergencies. Every day is a roll of the dice for the 911 squad, as it is called. The on-call possibilities are endless, running the gamut from a stolen bicycle to a high-speed chase. Those who can't handle the pressure or think quickly on their feet need not apply.

In early 1992, Danièle moved into plainclothes work. She became a part of the drug and morality squad and entered the murky Montreal drug scene. Typically, it wasn't a role most women would choose. Just like the law and order shows on TV, there were stakeouts, raids, and heart-stopping encounters in five-star hotels and dark back alleys. The work demanded sang-froid, the coolness and calmness of a 007.

Danièle spent five years exploring the seedy underside of her favourite city. There were moments of high drama along the way: busting a cop car filled with drug dealers, standing toe-to-toe with a gun-wielding outlaw wondering if and when he would reach for the trigger, leading a raid on a house knowing the fate of the double agent inside lay in her hands.

She tells the story about a covert operation in a high-end hotel. "This was a big drug case. We were tracking the moves of one of the big-time boys. He'd booked into a posh hotel downtown. I was staked out in the lobby, dressed very fashionably so I'd fit right in with the clientele. My job was to follow this guy's moves while my team upstairs worked on his room. He'd come down for dinner, or so we thought, but he stopped at reception, talked to someone and was now returning to the elevator. I knew I had to get to him before those doors opened, or our cover was blown. I sidled up to him and said in a sultry voice: 'I can do you favours.' My heart was pounding. 'Anything you want, I am sure I can provide. And, I am not that expensive.' The agent that was working the lobby with me knew immediately something was wrong. He radioed the guys upstairs and let them know it was time to get out. Thankfully, things worked out. To do this job, you have to stay cool and think fast."

The work appealed to Danièle. Unlike a uniformed officer responding to emergencies, plainclothes policing involved working on a file, or investigation, from A to Z. "It is a matter of putting all the pieces of the puzzle together, and that takes planning," says Danièle. "Sometimes, there is only one piece missing. You have to be determined to find it."

As she was discovering in her blossoming hockey career, dollars can sometimes alter the best-laid plans. "Investigations cost money, and sometimes the cold hard cash isn't there. You learn to get the best out of the resources available." The lessons learned dealing with life's darker side would serve her well in the hockey world.

Five years after starting with the Montreal city police, Danièle was promoted to sergeant. Just as her precocity in coaching had moved her quickly up the hockey ladder, she had demonstrated a natural bent for policing, too. Twelve years is the average span of experience for an aspiring sergeant. Danièle had more than halved that standard. The steps to promotion include an interview and an examination. The applicant needs to be thoroughly versed in a variety of areas from the Criminal Code and community police work to public relations, union policies and police procedures.

In 1996, not long after her promotion to sergeant, Danièle was seconded by the RCMP to work for a year on an international drug case. The investigation also involved the U.S. Drug Enforcement Agency and Interpol, the European counterpart. She has fond memories of that time: "I was going back to my first love, back to the police force that trained me. I felt very privileged. This was my first opportunity to work on an international drug case and see the resources that could be summoned. I saw, first hand, the long-term side to drug investigations. It takes years to bring a case to court. By the end of that year, I had become very proficient in long-term planning and investigation. This was an essential skill

Sergeant Sauvageau pictured in her Montreal Urban Community Police Service uniform.
(Bob Fisher, Montreal Canadiens)

that I would take with me to the hockey world."

For Danièle, there was one constant in her investigative work over the years. Rarely did unforeseen policing duties keep her away from the rink. Somehow, with clockwork precision, she'd always appear. Many were the times she'd walk into a practice or a game having just completed a two-day stakeout with no sleep. Thérèse Brisson, a national team member who played club hockey in the early nineties under Danièle, spoke of her dedication in the CHA's 2002 edition of *Pride and Passion*: "You would never have known she hadn't slept for forty-eight hours. It was quite incredible she was able to do that over those years. It's something I admire a lot." Louis Robitaille was equally impressed with his coach's ability to blend two careers during her time with the Rocket. "Danièle always came to practice with a smile on her face," he said.

In September of 1996, Sauvageau moved to Calgary to work with the women's high performance program and to prepare for the 1997 World's. She approached her superiors for her first extended leave of absence. "I was surprised at the response," she says. "They were very supportive. I've probably lived in Calgary a total of four years since then to pursue my coaching career at the national level. The Montreal police have backed me all the way. To represent my country at the Olympics has been the highest honour, and they respect and support this."

The relationship between coaching and policing has worked to the benefit of both parties. "Both professions are all about people management," says Danièle. "To build an Olympic team or an undercover team, it's all the same. Either way, you work with people."

The toughest juggling act of all came in 1999 when Danièle joined the staff of the Montreal Rocket. In the beginning, she could not have envisioned the subsequent sacrifices she'd have to make in her personal life. "I was working eighty-hour weeks, heading off to the arena when my shift was done," she says. "I had no time for family and friends. I had no social life at all." Still, this was a decision she doesn't regret. Hockey and policing were opposite ends of her teeter-totter. "One thing I've always been able to do," she says, "is to keep policing and hockey entirely separate. When I work as an officer, that's all I think about. When I am at the rink, I am totally focused on hockey. The two never cross over. One has been my break from the other."

Of all the lessons learned, it's her policing work, especially her time in undercover, that has helped Danièle put hockey in its proper perspective. "When you have life and death decisions to make, you begin to realize hockey is only a game. As a coach, you can't minimize too much the pressure the girls are under, but sometimes you have to make them see this too."

As the year 2000 rolled around, Salt Lake City was starting to come into view. Danièle didn't know it yet, but her policing career would soon be on hold once again. A perspective shaped by years devoted to seeing justice served would be a source of strength for the journey ahead.

After her shift was done, Danièle headed for the hockey rink.
(CP Picture Archive Vellis Krooks)

CHAPTER 9
On the Road to Salt Lake City

"Life is too short to live for one moment."

— Danièle Sauvageau

ON JULY 22, 2000, the CHA issued the announcement that would direct the course of Danièle's life for the next two years. Sauvageau would be the commander-in-chief for the march to the Olympics in 2002. Her assistants would be Melody Davidson and Wally Kozak. The mission was clear-cut: bring the gold medal to Canadian soil.

The challenge was formidable, but one Danièle was ready for. She took a leave of absence from the Montreal police service for twenty-two months and immersed herself in the task at hand. With Napoleonic fervour, Danièle began laying the groundwork for the campaign. The master strategist, noted in hockey circles as a meticulous planner, knew one thing: "No matter the outcome," she said, "I wanted to be at peace with myself." To reach this state, she was determined not to leave a single stone unturned. Karen Hughes, for one, didn't doubt for a minute her ability to pull this monumental undertaking together. "She is a visionary," Hughes said. "She looks down the road to the end and sees the way."

Directing the campaign meant moving to Calgary, the administrative hub of hockey in Canada. Of greater importance to Danièle, the town had the facilities and people to help bring her vision to fruition. The infrastructure and the

Danièle is appointed head coach for the run to Salt Lake City. Tom Renney presents her with her new jersey.   (CHA Archives)

experts who were drawn to this place in the foothills of the Rockies were a legacy of the 1988 Winter Olympics hosted here. The National Training Centre in Calgary was staffed with some of the best brains in the country in the sport science fields of physiology, nutrition, psychology, and strength and conditioning.   In her vision, Danièle would utilize their expertise to a level unprecedented in Canadian hockey, or most other sports for that matter.

Hockey, with its century-old history in Canada, was steeped in traditions and hidebound ways of thinking. Danièle brought a unique approach to the game. As a coach who had played but a few games of organized hockey, her perspective was shaped by her life experiences: as a ten-year-old at the end of the bench cracking the whip on her brothers' team; as a seventeen-year-old teenager coaching the boys' and girls' broomball teams at her college; as an RCMP recruit-in-training at The Depot; as a cop, on the beat and undercover, seeing the darker side of life in Montreal; as a keen observer of human behaviour fascinated by how people think and what they do. It was also a perspective borne out of a passion for hockey and an insatiable desire to learn as much as she could about the game. She would bring creativity to her vision, a way of thinking outside the box. She would train her players hard, but she would train them differently. A three-week training camp held in Val Cartier, Quebec, would be a model for doing things differently.

Finally, her vision would have a humanist's touch. There are technical, tactical and training sides to building a team. Danièle's vision encompassed a fourth dimension. She knew that, over time and with patience, all of the parts would come together if the human side was well looked after. The lens she looked through to see her team brought into focus twenty individuals with different strengths, needs and wants. Each would have a role to play in working toward the common goal: bringing home gold. When Sauvageau tapped a number on the back of a sweater, the player hopping over the boards had to believe in herself and believe in her teammates. When it counted most out on the ice, players had to take responsibility for themselves and their game. In her vision, team building was just as critical as stops and starts and a polished breakout.

Danièle knew the CHA had Olympic gold in mind when it hired her. This didn't alter her way of thinking. For her, the journey was key, not the destination. She made this clear from the outset. "Life is too short to live for one moment," she said.

"We are working on a process that will get us to Salt Lake City. It will lead us toward there, but we are taking it step by step." Gaetan Robitaille, the CHA's general manager of the women's high performance program and on-board with women's ice hockey since 1998, echoed her sentiments. "If we pay attention to the process, the outcome will be there." It took three months, but with Davidson and Kozak in tow, the team of three drew up the blueprint for 2002.

Melody Davidson had a long history of experience with coaching and with the women's national team. Her coaching career began in the tiny town of Oyen, Alberta (population 1,000). Like so many young girls in the seventies, playing hockey in a league wasn't an option, so she turned to coaching. "I think they got tired of seeing me around the rink, so they made me a coach," she says.

Her first national level appointment came in 1994 as an assistant at the world championships in Lake Placid, New York. Her first head coach appointment came 1998 with the first under twenty-two team which won the Christmas Cup in Europe. In 1999, she was the person in the eye of the storm when she replaced Sauvageau for a year as head coach, bringing Canada its sixth world championship in Mississauga, Ontario. In 1997, she took a year's leave to study at the University of Calgary's National Coaching Institute. When an American school came calling, she headed south and started the hockey program at Connecticut College. She guided the Division 3 team in the NCAA for three years. For the Canadian team heading to Salt Lake City, she would focus her expertise on defence and penalty killing.

If there were any problems with her appointment as assistant to Danièle Sauvageau for the Olympic run after a year at the helm, Davidson, the consummate team player, never let on. "I knew when I was appointed in 1999 that it was for one year. The CHA gave me a chance. It was their decision to appoint Danièle Olympic head coach and I accept that fully."

For Wally Kozak, the final member of the triumvirate, coaching coursed through his blood. He played with Ken Dryden, the great Canadiens goalie of the eighties, for one year on the national team in the late sixties but, since then, had devoted his energies to amassing a bucketful of coaching experience. His portfolio was as diverse and colourful as an artist's palette: Alberta Junior Hockey, the Western Hockey League, the Canadian Intercollegiate Athletic Union, the Spengler Cup, Alberta's Oval X-treme. He'd coached at all levels. At Nagano, he acted as mentor coach to the Japanese national women's team, culminating a four-year coaching stint in that country. He'd worked under Dave King, long-standing coach of the Canadian men's national team, as a skill and tactical specialist. This was the role he'd play on the women's team, working primarily with the forwards and on the power play. The assignment excited him. "We're hoping to really raise the bar offensively," he noted. "The female game allows you to do that. It's not consumed by the use of body checking, like the male game is. Puck possession, puck control, puck movement, offensive support, timing and execution—we've spent a lot more time on these things than guys' teams in North America."

How would three distinctly different personalities with diverse approaches come together? For Danièle, the answer was simple. "We'll talk a lot. The key thing is to talk." Kozak admits it wasn't always easy. "We had three people, each of whom was accustomed to being a head coach," he says. "In the beginning, we cracked heads a lot but, over time, we sorted things out. I have the utmost respect for Danièle. She didn't always agree with me, but she always let me have my say."

The journey to Salt Lake began with a sixty-eight-player developmental camp in Calgary in August 2000, then a thirty-four-player evaluation camp in October. These camps laid the groundwork for two major competitions to come: the Four Nations Cup in Provo, Utah, in November 2000 and the World Championships in Minneapolis, Minnesota, in April 2001.

The first event was a dry run for the Olympics, held at the Peaks Arena, one of two venues for ice hockey in the upcoming Olympics. Sweden, Finland and the U.S. were the other countries taking part. Canada hit the road running with a 2–0 victory over the States in the gold-medal game. It was an auspicious debut in their run for gold at Salt Lake City.

Danièle had arranged for a second team to be part of the proceedings in Provo. The team of sport scientists from the National Training Centre in Calgary were at the event. While the girls played, they gathered data. This marked the start of a detailed, multi-pronged program to prepare the team for the altitude in Salt Lake City. One of the key initiatives, driven by exercise physiologist Dr. Steve Norris and team physician Dr. Suzanne Leclerc, was doing blood work on each of the players. The objective was to assess the players' overall health including, most importantly, their iron status. Iron is an essential component of the blood. A low level of iron affects an individual's ability to deal with stress effectively. Iron also factors into the production of red blood cells, which carry oxygen through the blood. A deficiency of iron means fewer red blood cells are produced. This is critical for the high-performance athlete, especially at higher altitudes where there is already less oxygen in the atmosphere. A diminished red blood cell count means the body is less efficient utilizing what oxygen is available, thus hindering performance and recovery time. Provo marked the first in a series of blood tests conducted by the sport science team over the ensuing seventeen months leading to Salt Lake.

The second big event lay Canada's record of six consecutive world championships on the line. The Canadians would once again play in front of a pro-American assemblage in Minneapolis, Minnesota. "Good preparation for the upcoming Olympics," Cassie Campbell said. "The pressure is on them to produce." The Canucks swept the preliminaries, meeting the red, blue and white in the final. The U.S. played hard, out-shooting the Canadians 35–18, but they couldn't come through on the scoreboard. Canada won 3–2 in overtime. Kim St-Pierre was a rock in the Canadian goal. Ben Smith, the American coach and a noted humourist in the W. C. Fields vein, declared after the loss, "They shouldn't call this game hockey, they should call it 'goalie.'" The national team's record of consecutive world championships remained intact and now totalled seven.

Since the Four Nation's Cup, close to forty players had been given a "look-see" on the big team. Five rookies played in the World's. For Danièle, the mix of veterans and youth was a vital ingredient to the Canadian success: "That's what we have to continue to do as a country, work with our young players to bring them to the national team. Our philosophy is that a player might have a spot on the national team, but players coming up who want to be on the team are encouraged to battle for it. That approach will maintain our strength." For the veterans, life at the top wasn't easy. Jayna Hefford, one of the veterans, reflected on the challenge. "I could never take my position for granted," she says. "There was always somebody pushing from behind. For them, it was like the old adage: you're only as good as your last game."

Before the World's in April, chinks had appeared in the Canadian armour. The 2001 calendar included a couple of tours, starting in January with a western swing against Sweden. Games were played in tiny Hanna, Alberta, then in British Columbia with stopovers in Cranbrook, Trail, Kelowna and Golden. Over five matches, the Swedes had been outgunned 33–3 by the goliath Canucks. The Canadians' promising start, however, soon came to a screeching halt. Two games against the Americans, one in Red Deer, Alberta, at the end of January and the other in the mile-high city, Denver, Colorado, in early February were fought to declare a winner in The Sports Network Challenge series. The Americans drew first blood, winning 5–4 in the opening match. The second bout was the preliminary to the NHL All-Star game taking place the next day. However, 9,562 patrons, the largest crowd ever to attend a women's hockey game in the U.S., watched the home team drop its northern neighbour 3–2.

Two consecutive losses to the Americans were enough ammunition. The press, always on the hunt for a good story, attacked. Sauvageau bore the brunt of their blows. The storylines raised an oft-repeated refrain. Was a man more qualified to coach? Did she have what it took to take the team to the top? Was hers a token appointment to keep the feminists at bay? The cynics and skeptics demanded an answer. Danièle, positive as ever, was quick to respond. "I've been around hockey all of my life. I think back to the time I was ten at the arena with my younger brothers. You learn a lot by watching."

Despite the admonitions, Danièle believed in herself. "I think I was born to coach. Hockey, soccer, basketball. What does it matter? I think I would excel as a coach in any of them. I get tremendous satisfaction in seeing my players do things well." Let the naysayers bray and the doubters doubt, she thought. Her RCMP training had taught her not to worry about those aspects of life she could not control, but to focus her energies on the things she could. She knew, in the end, what had to be done: "I had to believe in myself and my plan."

CHAPTER 10

The Val Cartier Camp

"When it matters most, the body will do what the mind tells it to do."

— Danièle Sauvageau

THE AMERICANS had centralized since the beginning of 2000. Big name sponsors Visa and Nike and government funding of $1 million had made this possible. The Canadians would not be coming together to train until August 2001, a scant six months before the Olympics. To play the catch-up game, Danièle had to be at her ingenious and creative best.

The Val Cartier camp was the ace up her sleeve. It happened in June 2001. By Danièle's account, this was the seminal event in her two-year plan, the one that produced Olympic gold.

Wally Kozak remembers his thinking when Danièle relayed to him her idea to hold a training camp at a military base. "It was a gutsy call. Nothing like this had been done in the hockey world before."

Val Cartier is a spot on the map forty kilometres north of Quebec City nestled in the eroded northern end of the Appalachian chain of mountains. For outdoor enthusiasts, a rabbit warren of mountain biking and cross-country ski trails make it an outdoor paradise. There is even a small downhill ski area for the telemarkers, snowboarders and alpine skiers. In actual fact, the town's *raison d'être* is the Canadian Forces army base located here. A spaghetti network of roads winds through the base facilities. The potpourri includes the command headquarters, gymnasium, swimming pool, arena, mess hall, barracks, other military buildings, and the tanks, jeeps and trucks that are part and parcel of the paraphernalia of military life. Quebec City, with its old-world ambience, lies a half hour to the south, overlooking the mighty St. Lawrence River.

A pool of thirty girls, twenty of whom would represent Canada in Salt Lake City, was selected after the World's in Minneapolis. The girls gathered in Val Cartier in early June to begin the most important three weeks of their training year. Drawing deeply from the well of experience The Depot had provided as an RCMP recruit-in-training, Danièle knew the process she was about to embark upon was not about developing hockey players; rather, it was about developing Olympic athletes. Her police training had taught her the importance of discipline, determination, responsibility and courage. At The Depot, she learned to handle adversity and work as a team. These were the qualities she wanted to instill in her team.

And so began a rigorous schedule of daily activities. The day began at 6:00 a.m. with breakfast in the mess hall. Mornings were devoted to hockey; there were two arenas on the base. One group of players rode seven kilometres on their bicycles, supplied by the base, to the rink where the on-ice workouts took place. Two specialists assisted the hockey staff: Lorraine Ostiguy worked with the players on power skating; Thomas Pacina conducted sessions on puck handling. At the other rink, the ice was out and the players ran on a concrete floor, working on off-ice stick handling and shooting under Wally Kozak. Half way through the morning, the groups switched sites.

There was a temporary reprieve for lunch, then afternoons devoted to dry-land training and outdoor pursuits, including running, cycling, rollerblading, tennis, racquetball, basketball, volleyball and swimming. An hour and a half cycling mountain trails under a searing sun, followed by a strength and conditioning session were as much an exercise in mind over matter as a gruelling workout. When it mattered most, Sauvageau believed, the body would do what the mind told it to do.

Dinner was at 6:00 p.m. back in the mess hall. Evenings were devoted to team building and martial arts exercises, including yoga, karate and taebo. Danièle believed these ancient arts would teach proper breathing techniques, develop discipline and quickness, and aid relaxation.

For thirty elite hockey players, handpicked as "the best of the best" in Canadian women's hockey, the daily adversity was a small price to pay for a shot at Olympic gold. The esprit de corps this camp fostered would be a source of strength, a well to draw on, when the chips were down; in short, perfect preparation for a gold medal game.

Jayna Hefford recalls her first day at camp. "I am not sure how many of us really wanted to be here, on an army base, and it was so hot. A group of us looked at the schedule of activities over the next three weeks. None of us believed we could accomplish half of what we were seeing, especially the eighty-kilometre bike ride that started one of the days. That's a long way for someone who doesn't normally ride a bike. Despite our doubts that first day, the camp was probably the most fun and rewarding challenge of the year. It was hard work, but we did everything. We learned a lot about ourselves and each other."

The highlight of camp was the obstacle course. The girls pushed aside the breakfast trays one morning and, instead of the rink, headed into the field. The Van Doos, a crackerjack army regiment like the Green Berets of the U.S., had constructed a set straight out of *Rambo*. It was a labyrinth of ropes, ladders, walls, ditches, tunnels and other impediments to travel, to be crawled under, climbed over or squeezed through. These military superstars had tested the course twice already that morning, even though the sun had barely touched the sky. Now, it was the girls' turn. They were divided into four teams, each commanded by a Van Doo. There were eighteen obstacles in total, eighteen Mount Everests to conquer. All were, as Wally Kozak declared, "life threatening." One required hanging, chimpanzee-like, ten feet above the ground, swinging from one rung of a horizontal rope ladder to the next. At another, the victim belly-wiggled through the dirt using her elbows as feet and, like a giant centipede, wormed her way under a rectangular array of crisscrossing ropes. Success was achieved only when each and every member of the team completed the stations.

Sauvageau was part of one team. She describes one memorable moment: "We had to climb a rope to get over a wall. One of the girls said to me, 'I'm afraid of heights. I can't do it.' I told her I would climb with her. Well, she got over the top and down the other side. 'Thanks,' she said. 'It was because of you that I did it.' I looked her in the eye and said: 'Always remember. You didn't do it for me. You did it for yourself.' I wanted these girls to believe in themselves."

For most of the players, evenings never lasted much beyond 9:00 p.m; 6:00 a.m. risings and long, tough days made bed in the barracks too enticing.

The veterans knew that living in close quarters was part of the Olympic experience, too. In Nagano, the players were housed eight to a suite: three in one room, three in the second and two in a tiny third. Three weeks of barracks living, with not much space and little privacy, would introduce the newcomers and remind the experienced players about what to expect from village life in Salt Lake City.

Sauvageau had earmarked Val Cartier as the place to come for intensive training for several reasons. Budgetary constraints had ruled out centralizing the team until August. Val Cartier would offer a very different look and feel to Calgary, the centralization site. Three weeks of living in the heart of Quebec, with Quebec City a stone's throw away, would be a snapshot of a different world for many of the players; a change of culture: "Like travelling to Europe

The Canadian players join with the army for a photo op at Val Cartier, Quebec. Denis Coderre, federal minister in charge of amateur sport, was instrumental in providing funding for the camp. (CFB Val Cartier Archives)

without crossing the ocean," Sauvageau said. Most importantly, the military base had top-of-the-line facilities, everything Sauvageau needed to implement her non-traditional training program. Plus, she had a contingent of army personnel dedicated to providing her with whatever support she needed.

Three weeks of time together with the group of athletes vying for Olympic spots was an immersion opportunity for Sauvageau, too, in her coaching role with her subjects at hand. Since her appointment, she and the athletes had come together in week-long stints for major events, like the Four Nations Cup and the World's. The Val Cartier camp was precious time to work, over a longer period, with her athletes and imprint her style.

For Sauvageau, coaching had always been equal parts art and science. She relied on her team of experts to provide information and to be a part of the decision-making process. But at the end of the day, the final decision was hers. Her most critical calls were a master's blend of fact and intuition. During the day, when the players were on the ice or in the gym, Sauvageau would be the observer watching, listening, reflecting on the unfolding action while her experts ran the show. The processing never stopped. In the evenings, sitting with the team in the common room, she was still the observer, keenly attentive to what was happening around her.

Danièle tells the story about one little game she played: "I had a crumpled piece of paper in my hands. When no-one was looking, I threw it into the middle of the floor. I wanted to see how long it would lie there, who would be the first to pick it up. After all, we were sharing this space together. I wondered who would feel responsible for keeping it clean. The way someone thinks and acts extends to the ice: who takes responsibility for herself and her teammates?"

Team building was a primary focus at the Val Cartier camp, while a second mandate was physical fitness. Dr. Steve Norris arrived from Calgary just as the camp was starting. He was a specialist in exercise physiology and had been on board with the team since the Four Nations Cup in Provo. His expertise would be an essential ingredient in preparing the girls for Salt Lake, as much of his adult life had been spent working with Olympic athletes. In addition to his academic posting in the Faculty of Kinesiology at the University of Alberta, he was one of two sport science directors at the Canadian Sports Centre in Calgary.

The other was his boss, Dr. David Smith. An Englishman by birth, he'd completed his undergraduate studies in London before moving to Canada to complete his master's and doctoral program at the University of Alberta. He had worked with high-performance athletes in the sliding and gliding sports since 1990. He relished the opportunity to head east and work with Danièle for three weeks. "She was a breath of fresh air," he says. "She's one of the few coaches I've come across who really allowed the sport scientists in Calgary to work very closely with her and develop a long-term strategy. Her plan wasn't something put in place overnight. She had a clear vision of how she wanted things to go and worked with us to get there."

Furthermore, Dr. Norris was impressed by the nimble footwork that enabled Danièle to circumvent the obstacles in her path. "We have what I call a gold, a silver and a bronze plan," he explains. "Financial pressures in the women's game can get in the way of preparation, turning a gold plan into something less. Danièle is a master at examining alternatives and working with her sport science people to come up with scaled-down solutions." Val Cartier was a prime example. Originally, Dr. Norris and his team had wanted the hockey team to centralize in Calgary in the spring of 2001. For budgetary reasons, this wasn't possible. Sauvageau's staging of the boot camp at Val Cartier became the gold plan alternative, an innovative approach to high volume training, far enough away from centralization in August and well out from Salt Lake City to be most effective.

Hockey is a game of short, sharp bursts of high intensity activity. Most shifts last thirty to forty seconds, then the player returns to the bench and waits for the next burst. The game, Dr. Norris says, was never designed by an exercise physiologist. "We would have the players skating on a sheet of ice behind the bench after their shift to taper down." To execute these shifts at the highest level, it was essential to develop the aerobic capacity or stamina of the players involved. "The players were all over the board in this regard," says Dr. Norris. "Some rated with the best Olympic athletes and others had very inflated notions of their aerobic capacity."

To aid in the training process, Dr. Norris brought two strength and conditioning experts with him, Jason Poole from the National Sport Training Centre in Calgary and Alain Delorme from the regional training facility in Montreal. A combination of dry-land training, on-ice workouts and outdoor pursuits would provide the very high volume of training necessary to build an aerobic base. Dr. Norris explains, "If we wanted to move to high-intensity training preparing for a series of games at the Olympics and the final toughest game of them all, presumably against the Americans, the athletes needed to have a physical work capacity within them to sustain that." In layperson's terms, they needed to have the physical conditioning to go hard, every shift, over sixty minutes of hockey, and they needed to have the stamina to physically perform at their optimum in every game spread over two weeks.

The Val Cartier camp, with its six to eight hours of varied activities each day, would do just that. When the players headed home for a month and a half before centralization, they'd be more than just hockey players; they'd be well on their way to becoming Olympic athletes.

CHAPTER *11*

The Psychology of Coaching

Like a Caramilk bar, hard on the outside,
soft on the inside.

TO COACH elite athletes at the highest level of competition requires years of preparation. In actual fact, Danièle began her preparation when she was a ten-year-old gatekeeper, standing by the bench at the only arena in Deux-Montagnes, watching her two younger brothers play hockey. The impetus to aspire to the highest level came almost two decades later at the first World's in 1990. From that moment, Danièle dedicated herself to becoming a national-level coach in women's hockey.

Twelve years later, she is one of an exclusive group in ice hockey, counting only seven women and twenty-two men, who have earned the appellation "master coach." Other names include her two assistants, Melody Davidson and Wally Kozak, and two presently working in the NHL, Dave King, head coach of the Columbus Blue Jackets, and Tom Renney, vice-president of player personnel with the New York Rangers. To attain this level demands determination, a commitment to excellence and years devoted to climbing up the rungs. The 3M National Coaching Certification Program, Levels 4 and 5, are the final rungs on the ladder, the PhD in coaching.

The process to completing Level 4 is long and arduous. Says Sauvageau, "Getting my Level 4 took more energy than my

undergraduate degree. There is more work to do and far more years of study to put in."

The admission requirements for Level 4 include experience in high-performance sport, meaning at the college, university, midget triple A, junior or national levels, and approval from the Canadian Hockey Association. There are twenty tasks in total to complete at Levels 4 and 5, twelve of which are required for Level 4. These include: energy-systems (meaning the way the human body utilizes energy and the byproducts of energy use), strength training for elite athletes, sport-specific performance factors (e.g. rest, downtime and high intensity training), psychological preparation for coaches and for elite athletes, skills training (e.g. skating, stick-handling, shooting), strategy and tactics (e.g. breakouts, power plays and penalty killing), planning and periodization (i.e. approaches to training over a year, including the preseason, the competitive season and the off-season), analyzing performance factors (more simply, team statistics like face-offs won and lost, power play goals and the efficiency of the penalty kill), practical coaching (running a training camp and participating in a competitive tour), and, finally, self-awareness and personal management (i.e. balancing the demands of coaching with life outside of hockey).

Every task involves the practical application of concepts learned. Instruction in tasks with extensive theoretical components like energy systems and psychological preparation is delivered by university professors, either through CHA-sanctioned seminars or at a national coaching institute or at Canadian universities offering Level 4 certification as part of a master's degree in coaching.

The final hurdle is the defence of her hockey thesis, which details a yearly training plan that the coach has followed, before a panel of experts in the relevant disciplines. The presentation must be supported by a printed version of the plan, usually a weighty tome several centimetres thick that outlines seasonal, technical, off-season and psychological plans. Simply stated, it is "Here is what I did, here is why I did it, here is how it worked and here is what I would do differently."

Most Level 4 coaches have invested at least ten to twenty years behind the bench, accumulating the practical experience that goes with the theory.

The first level, "coach," covers the rudiments of coaching a hockey team, which every individual standing behind a bench directing a team needs to know. Most people spend at least two years gaining experience before tackling the next rung, the intermediate level. Unlike coach, this level includes a theoretical as well as technical and practical components.

Advanced 1 and Advanced 2 follow with one requirement layered in between, Theory 3. This is a twenty-eight-hour course delivered outside the hockey program through the universities. The Advanced 2 course covers a one-week practical component involving classroom work; in addition, there is field work and an examination. When Advanced 2 and Theory 3 are completed, the aspiring master coach can move on to Level 4.

Sauvageau has begun the process that will take her to the even more rarefied air of the Level 5 coach. Cindy Flett, overseer of the Women in Coaching Program implemented by Sport Canada, has been a pillar of support for Danièle and other aspiring female coaches over the years. With Flett's encouragement and initiatives, Danièle has completed four of the eight remaining tasks leading to certification as the absolute best of the best; nutrition for optimal performance, athlete long-term development, leadership skills and national team programme are the dragons she has already slain in her assault on Level 5.

At the end of the journey, the master coach is thoroughly schooled in the five pillars of high level athletic performance. These are tactics and strategy, biomechanics, physiology, psychology, and health and nutrition. The end goal for years of study, performance, assessment and evaluation for Danièle was to work with athletes who had the potential to perform at an Olympic level.

As she gained experience at the national level, it became increasingly evident to her that an Olympic-calibre athlete needs to be a well-grounded athlete, not only gifted athletically, but also able to handle the stressors on and off the ice. Travel, finances, diet, fatigue, media, family, friends and significant others can all impact adversely on performance. The psychological stability needed to deal with the rigours of daily training, to "dig deep" when it counts the most and to compete under conditions that are less than perfect, is an essential component to becoming an Olympic athlete.

Says Danièle, "When the gold medal is on the line, an athlete's mental state determines the difference. Self-esteem is the key. I use the analogy of the hockey puck. A player wants it. When she gets it, she wants to keep it. When she loses it, she wants it back. The same is true for self- esteem. A player wants to feel good about herself. When she doesn't, she wants to get that feeling back. An athlete, above all else, must believe in herself. To have high self-esteem, four things must happen. The athlete needs to feel important, capable, confident and competent."

A favourite illustration relates to her RCMP days. "When I finished my training at The Depot," Danièle begins, "they gave me a gun. That was a very powerful symbol for me. The RCMP gave me this huge responsibility because they believed that, at the end of six months, I now had the training and the judgment to use it wisely.

"The girls on the national team are each given a role. They, too, have to be willing to accept the responsibility that goes along with that role. They have to believe in themselves, that they have the training and the skill to fulfill that responsibility. The strength to handle high-performance situations has to come from within. This comes back to self-esteem. Players need to feel confident in the decisions they make."

Melding twenty distinctly different individuals into a team is a herculean task at the best of times. To coax an Olympic performance out of that team raises the bar to another level.

Many of Danièle's team-building tasks revolved around one word—respect. She uses the Thomas concept, more commonly known as the performance iceberg, to explain her thinking: "So often, we base our perceptions about a person on what we see on the surface, how a person looks, how she dresses, what she says, how she behaves. So much about this person is hidden from view, like the biggest part of an iceberg. The vision, the interests, the values, the needs and the wants are not there, in full view, for us to see; they are the most important elements in understanding someone else. We need to look beneath the surface to really see what someone is all about. Only in this way can we understand people and their differences and learn to respect them.

"Take athletes under pressure, for example. Some want to laugh; some to cry; some want to be by themselves or be with others. There is nothing wrong with any of that. Differences are okay. We focus a lot in team-building on learning not to judge, but to accept and respect each other's differences."

To assist in getting to know her athletes better, Danièle accessed another invaluable resource—the parents. To have them on board was essential. "So often," she explains, "those closest to us have the most influence." The parents' involvement was a two-way street: Danièle could educate them on the needs of Olympic athletes and the parents, in turn, could educate her on factors outside the cocoon of the team that, potentially, could have an impact on a daughter's performance. To facilitate communications, three regional parent "captains" were appointed, one for each of the three regional training centres in Calgary, Toronto and Montreal. Each captain would relay team information down the line to other parents in the area. The flow was aided and abetted by a parent newsletter.

A long-standing practice, initiated by Danièle at the World's in 2001, was to invite the parents into the dressing room approximately three hours prior to game time. "This really made them feel a part of the process," points out Danièle. "They could talk to the athletes, relax and support them. They would carry the mental image of the girls getting ready back up to the stands for the start of the game. For the players, it was a comforting feeling to know ahead of time where their parents were sitting."

To help with the psychological side of high-level performance, Danièle called upon Kimberley Amirault to join her team of experts. Still in her late twenties, Amirault had already amassed an impressive curriculum vitae. She was director of sports psychology at the Canadian Sport Centre in Calgary and adjunct assistant professor in the Faculty of Kinesiology and the Division of Applied Psychology at the University of Calgary. At the 2002 Games, she'd work with both the women's ice hockey and the cross-country ski teams. Born in the Maritimes, she'd completed her undergraduate studies at Mount Allison in psychology and her master's at the University of Ottawa in sport psychology. She decided if she wanted to work with Olympic athletes, Calgary was the place to be and that's were she headed for her PhD program. She completed her doctoral studies at the University of Calgary in counselling psychology, specializing in working with elite athletes. In addition to her responsibilities at the university and with Olympic teams, she also acts as the sport psychologist for two professional teams, the New York Rangers of the National Hockey League and the New York Knicks of the National Basketball Association.

Dr. Amirault's work with the women's ice hockey team was broadly focused: confidence issues, stress management, the handling of distractions, visualization of positive outcomes and relaxation. Having pockets of time together with the players, like the week she spent at Val Cartier, enabled Amirault to work closely with Danièle to co-ordinate a meaningful program. Says Amirault, "Danièle was great at communicating team objectives. She would go so far as to invite me to join some of the coaches' meetings. This really helped me develop strategies that were in synch with the team's goals."

The team spent much of the 2001 season on the road. Vicky Sunohara, for one, found the relaxation sessions a boon for the body and the mind. "A lot of us had trouble sleeping on the road," she offered. "Even though we were exhausted, long after a game, hockey sticks were in our minds. Dr. Amirault would conduct sessions to help us relax. We'd lie on the floor with the lights out, and then she'd have us do some visualization. I'd last maybe ten minutes before I'd fall asleep."

Team building started seriously in May 2001 when the pool of players selected for centralization met in Calgary for a week. In one of those sessions, Amirault had the players brainstorm for the one word that would guide their Olympic quest and point the way for the rest of the journey. A verbal outpouring ensued, unabated, for the next half hour to find the word that would best describe their team to the outside world. Amirault scribbled furiously on her overhead. Loyal, disciplined, committed, fun and hardworking were some of the words that made the list. As the descriptors piled up, she altered the exercise. "Give me an acronym," she instructed. Some minutes later, the word WAR reverberated through the room. "WE ARE RESPONSIBLE," someone shouted.

"It came out of Nagano," Sunohara explains. "The veterans from those Olympics remembered the aftermath and the excuses. Players were saying we should have done this, we should have done that. We didn't want Salt Lake to end the same way. This time, we would be responsible for everything we could control and deal with the things we couldn't. There would be no excuses, no regrets, no laying the blame on someone or something else."

The peaceful WAR had the desired effect. Every time someone lost focus, the three-letter word was the cue to bring mind and body back to the task.

A second team-building exercise late in 2001 had a similarly profound effect. Dr. Amirault, touring with the team on the

Maritime swing in December, interviewed each and every team member heading to Salt Lake City. The task she set related to individuals this time: tell me one positive thing, in a word or a phrase, about each of your teammates, your coaches and your support staff. She gathered a basket of golden nuggets for each individual and recorded the offerings on laminated card stock. At a team meeting in Gander, Newfoundland, each person was introduced by another using the list of attributes that filled her card. The catchiest offering of all that afternoon appeared on the card of Coach Sauvageau: like a caramel bar, hard on the outside, soft on the inside. The Caramilk bar was renown for disguising its soft interior. The ex-undercover agent had challenged her players in many ways. Was this yet another?

For Sunohara, the card about her included words like funny, good-humoured, social and a good leader. It would be her talisman for the rest of the journey. "So often," she says, "when you're playing or practising, you dwell on your negatives. My card reminded me, every day, of my positive qualities."

Over time, Dr. Amirault would deal with many of the players on an individual basis as their needs dictated. Once centralized in Calgary, Amirault's base, the players had ready access to her services. As well, she travelled with the team on its road trips leading up to the Olympics. Her age and youthful exuberance helped ease her admittance into the circle of hockey players. Hanging out in airports with the team, gauging the mood in the dressing room before games and between periods and observing practices gave Amirault a bird's eye view on the ups and downs of an Olympic athlete. Her professional expertise, in both formal and informal settings, became a key cog in the performance wheel. Sauvageau, for one, was delighted to have her on board. After all, was there a better sounding board for someone certain the path to Olympic glory lay in mind over matter?

CHAPTER 12
Centralization

"Only the bounces make the difference."

— Ben Smith, Head Coach, Team U.S.A.

ON AUGUST 5, the thirty women who'd disbanded after the Val Cartier camp were reunited in Calgary, Alberta, for the start of an intensive six months of training. They'd left jobs, family, friends and significant others behind to focus their existence on hockey. Even the handful who lived in Calgary would leave the familiar routine of their daily lives behind to become part of an exclusive band dedicated to the pursuit of hockey gold.

Calgary is the site of a Canadian Training Centre and one of five regional Centres of Excellence for hockey across the country. The others are located in Saint John, New Brunswick; Vancouver, British Columbia; Mississauga, Ontario; and Montreal, Quebec. The selection of Calgary for centralization was a natural given that the CHA headquarters are located here with offices in the Father David Bauer Arena.

Father David Bauer had been a key figure in the development of the men's national program for more than thirty years. The rink that bore his name had welcomed many national teams over the years, and it would be the venue six days a week, six to eight hours a day, for on-ice workouts and strength and conditioning programs for the women.

The Canadian Training Centre in Calgary also came equipped with a highly skilled team of sport science professionals who, in close consultation with Danièle, would implement a diverse approach to the intensive training that lay ahead. This would include fitness, weight training, nutrition, psychology, physiology and biomechanics. The "team" was equal to the challenge. As Dr. Steve Norris said, "We work with Olympic athletes all day, every day."

Danièle had worked closely with Dr. Norris and the rest of his team since assuming the mantle of head coach, including the intensive three-week interlude at Val Cartier. She understood their language and valued their expertise, developing a level of trust in the working relationship well beyond that of most coach-sport science staff collaborations.

The Canadian team had centralized in Calgary once before. That was prior to the '98 Olympics in Nagano. Twelve members of the present squad had been a part of that experience. For the eighteen others, this was something new.

Everyone had come to Calgary in May for a week to do physical testing and find a place to live during centralization. All were eager to get started. Once settled in, the business of hockey was all that was on their minds. "Most of us have jobs that go along with commitments to the national team and our club teams," said Cassie Campbell, "but now, we're full-time hockey players."

The makeup of the thirty invitees included four goaltenders, ten defencewomen and sixteen forwards. The Olympic roster would consist of twenty players, eighteen skaters and two goalies. All would know by November 20, 2001, when the Olympic team was named, whether or not they'd reached their goal. Changes in the lineup were still possible until January 14, 2002.

Centralization was the final kick in the stretch run to the Olympics. It would give Danièle and her staff time to implement systems, work on special teams, familiarize the players with each other, form lines, develop team cohesion and

(CHA Archives)

The centralization squad and staff pictured on the ice in Calgary.

close whatever physiological gap existed between them and the Americans who had been together in Lake Placid since November 2000.

The resident-team approach underpinned the U.S. national team development program. The first long bout of U.S. centralization occurred prior to Nagano to prepare for those Olympics. The team had come together for varying periods of time thereafter.

The Canadians had taken a different route. The reasons were one part budgetary, one part philosophical. More often than not, the Canadian team would come together a week or so before major tournaments like the Four Nations Cup and the World Championships to practise. Tours and developmental and evaluation camps were the common vehicles for player selection.

The three regional centres in Montreal, Mississauga and Calgary, which represented the home bases of most players, were used extensively for training purposes. For example, when the players returned to their homes for a month and a half after Val Cartier and before centralization, each reported three times a week to her training centre for a supervised workout under the watchful eye of a strength and conditioning coach. If blood work was needed by the sport science people in Calgary, players would access their family physicians to do the testing.

At the core of the difference in the Canada–U.S. approach to national team development lies the strength of Canada's club system. Without exception, every member of the Canadian team plays on a Senior A up to AAA club team, the most competitive level there is in women's hockey, with a rigorous schedule of games over the season. In Ontario alone, there is a plethora of strong teams vying for provincial and national honours. The Beatrice Aeros have won the provincial championship six years running, nine times in the nineties alone. Victory is never easy, with strong opposition from teams like the Mississauga Ice Bears, the Brampton Thunder and the

Ottawa Raiders. The national championship is always a high-profile, hotly contested affair garnering lots of media and public attention. The top teams across the country, the Oval X-treme out of Calgary, plus the Edmonton Chimos, the Vancouver Griffins, the Montreal Wingstar, the Telus Lightning and Le Cheyenne ooze national talent on their rosters.

The number of registered hockey players in the country has swelled more than 800% since 1990. Back then, just over 7,000 females played on sanctioned teams; today, the number has ballooned to well over 60,000, each player wearing the crest of one of more than 5,000 club teams. The number of elite players has risen in consort with the growth of hockey at the grassroots level. Many of today's stars—Campbell, Heaney, Sunohara, Brisson, Wickenheiser, to name a few—are now part of the National Women's Hockey League (NWHL), the development of which was spearheaded by, among others, France St-Louis after her retirement in 1999.

Today, St-Louis owns and administers the Wingstar, spawned from Ferland 4-Glace, the Montreal team she played on with Sauvageau as coach in the early nineties. The NWHL, comprised originally from teams in Quebec and Ontario, has spread westward, adding to its ranks the two Alberta-based powerhouses, the Oval X-treme and the Chimos, as well as the Griffins from Vancouver. The American icon, Cammie Granato, has committed to the Vancouver team for the 2002 season leading the flow of tier one American talent north. St-Louis has high hopes for the league and what it can do for women's hockey careers. "By 2005 or 2006 at the outset, we'd like to have a professional league in the true sense of the word, meaning women are getting paid to play hockey, just like the National Women's Basketball Association in the States. It takes time to build a big enough talent base, but we're getting there."

For highly talented young players choosing to further their academic careers, there is the Canadian university system with the Canadian Intercollegiate Athletic Union national championship serving as the pot of gold at the end of the rainbow, or the American college route. Canadian Jennifer Botterill plays on the perennial NCAA championship contender, the Harvard Crimson Tide, and was named player of the year in the NCAA in 2001. Tammy Lee Shewchuck is the Crimson Tide's all-time leading scorer. Teammate Isabelle Chartrand attended school at St. Lawrence University in New York state for a year. Dana Antal is a Cornell grad. Becky Keller was a most valuable player with Brown University, another Ivy League school. Sami Jo Small played in goal for the men's team and obtained her degree in mechanical engineering at Stanford, one of the top-ranked academic schools in the States. All are current-day national team members.

In Team Canada games versus Team U.S.A., these collegians often play against American teammates from their college squads. Sauvageau has no problem with Canadian players getting some of their coaching with club teams or south of the border. "Other coaches have things to offer too," she says. "By putting our players in different situations, like in college or in club hockey, it only makes them better. They play for different coaches. Jennifer Botterill has only become a better player in college."

A typical day in Calgary began at 9:00 a.m. when the players arrived at Father David Bauer Arena for a two-hour on-ice workout. There was a break for lunch, then afternoon sessions devoted to dry land training at the Calgary Oval, lifting weights and spinning countless kilometres on the stationary bicycles. Sometimes, players reassembled in the evenings for yoga sessions or team meetings. For Vicky Sunohara and the other players, the time passed quickly. "I shared a house with Lori Dupuis and Jayna Hefford. Hayley Wickenheiser's parents, who live in Calgary, actually found it for us back in May. It was a short walk to the rink. Unlike the American players who stayed together in a residence in Lake

Placid, we got to pick our roommates and live on our own. It was nice to have a life away from the other players and away from the rink for part of the day."

In addition to training, most of the players completed the first two levels of the coaching certification program during their time in Calgary. It was an initiative introduced by assistant coach Mel Davidson. Over the long term, she saw this as a potential career path for retired national team players and a way to involve more women in hockey coaching.

There was no time outside of hockey to earn an income. All of the players were senior carded athletes under the Athlete Assistance Program funded by Sport Canada. As such, each received a monthly stipend of $1,100 to cover her living and training needs. Any additional income was generated from savings accumulated while working prior to centralization or depended on the largesse of parents or others.

Early in October, the national squad left its training base and hit the road. For all, the change of pace was a welcome relief from the tedium of training. The team swung through British Columbia with matches against Sweden in Victoria, Campbell River and Port Alberni. The young and inexperienced Swedish side provided little opposition for the savvy, talent-laden Canadians. Although the outcome was never in doubt in any match, with scores of 10–0, 7–0 and 10–0 respectively, the Canadian girls were a *cause célèbre* on every tour stop along the way. Many in the crowds that gathered to see them play were young females, obviously excited about the game and their heroes who played it so skillfully.

The national players take their role as ambassadors for women's hockey very seriously. In this, the road trips gave the players a chance to shine. Fifteen hundred leather-lunged fans filled the rink in tiny Hanna, Alberta, where Hayley Wickenheiser, herself a native of a small prairie town— Shaunavon, Saskatchewan—scored her fiftieth goal as a national team member.

Danièle explains a tactic to Cassie Campbell.   (CP Picture Archive Vellis Krooks)

Hayley's career on the national team began in 1994, at the tender age of fifteen. A fierce competitor, highly skilled, tall and powerful and with a will of iron, she's been a star ever since. Wickenheiser is widely regarded as the best female hockey player on the planet, the complete package. Her stint at a NHL Philadelphia Flyers training camp is well documented. Plus, her three-Olympic status, in summer fastball at Sydney and winter hockey at Nagano and Salt Lake, and her attempt to crack men's professional hockey with a European team only add fodder to her near-mythic persona.

The Cranbrook Colonels old-timers organized the arrival of Team Canada to their town for the second of five games against the Swedes. The event covered the front page of the hometown weekly and raised a substantial sum for the local hospital. Even in the bigger centres, like Copps Coliseum in Hamilton or the Corel Centre in Ottawa, the games drew an enthusiastic, vocal crowd of loyal supporters. Young girls lined the corridor leading to the dressing room, awaiting autographs from their hockey idols, many dreaming of a chance to perform on the national and Olympic stage some day.

The game has lots to sell. Unlike their male counterparts, the women are not allowed to deliver the bone-crunching body checks into the glass like their NHL brethren. There are no obvious assaults in front of the net. Hooking and holding, rampant in the pros, are not a part of the women's game. The result is a fast, flowing, open game where skating and hockey skills, like passing and stick handling and playing a team game, are showcased.

Cassie Campbell is the other poster girl, next to Hayley Wickenheiser, on the national scene. Cassie's face once graced cereal boxes across the country. She first appeared on the national scene in 1994 and has played in more than one hundred games for her country since. More than just a high-profile hockey player and a pretty face, she's an advocate for smoking prevention for young girls and for the CHA Speak Out Campaign against harassment and abuse. In addition, she sponsors a community school, Applewood Acres, for the intellectually and physically challenged.

Both Hayley and Cassie's public presence is enhanced by their efforts to promote women's hockey at the grassroots level. In the summer of 2001, Hayley Wickenheiser crossed the nation with her one-on-one hockey clinics designed to teach the basics to young girls, as well as older women. Female hockey players are sprouting like dandelions in June in Prince Edward Island thanks to Cassie Campbell's hockey schools. Statistics indicate that more girls play hockey per capita in P.E.I. than any other province in the country. Jayna Hefford and Lori Dupuis have run hockey schools, aptly named Olympic Bound, in Kingston and Ottawa, Ontario, for years. As France St-Louis, who has turned her hockey playing days into a career running hockey schools in Quebec, says, "It's not just the youngsters who want to play. I have adults asking me all the time: 'Where can I learn to skate? How can I develop my skills?'"

Despite the successes, and the obvious passion for the game the elite players possess, these women's rise to the top often came at great sacrifice to personal and professional lives.

Thérèse Brisson sacrificed years of working toward her doctorate in kinesiology and garnering a university posting in pursuit of hockey's grail—Olympic gold; she left her professorship at the University of New Brunswick to pursue her hockey dreams.

Vicky Sunohara first made the national team in 1990. Over the decade, she was cut from the team twice, in 1992 and 1994, before cracking the lineup for Nagano in 1998. The last four years were devoted to a second Olympic appearance. "My friends have houses, good jobs, families," she says. "I don't regret my decision though. My passion is hockey."

Geraldine Heaney is the most decorated women's hockey player ever with the most long-standing record of service at the national level. When she started out at age seven, she was the only girl in a boys' league, and the boys didn't make it easy for her; however, her love for the game overcame all obstacles and she stuck with hockey, ignoring the taunts. Her national career began in 1990 with the first World's. She is the only Canadian to have played in all seven world championships, she's competed in every Three and Four Nations Cup, she went to Nagano and she's on board for Salt Lake City. All the while, she's supplemented her hockey career working in recreation in the Toronto area. Still the financial sacrifices were worth it. She'd travelled the world, met all kinds of people and played a game she loved to play.

Danielle Goyette, another veteran member with ten years' experience at the highest level, endured twenty-three dislocations to her shoulder and surgery, too, to play the game. Four years ago, the doctor said she should stop playing hockey. It was advice she never heeded.

Jennifer Botterill postponed her last year of school at Harvard to prepare for and play in an Olympic year. Although working on a degree in psychology, there was no question in my mind that she would devote 2001 to hockey.

Ditto for Kim St-Pierre, the goalie who put her year at McGill on hold to pursue her Olympic dream. Other youngsters, like Cherie Piper, age twenty and not long out of high school, resigned themselves to living at home and sacrificing the accoutrements that are standard fare for others their age if that's what it took to play at the top.

Sauvageau put a "normal" life on hold for a decade in the pursuit of her dream. "I've sacrificed a lot," she admits, "to be where I am today: family, friends, social life, even my policing career. Still, I feel privileged. Not lucky. Luck is buying a Lotto 649 card and winning. I've worked very hard to get where I am today."

In late October, Team Canada was on the road again. This time, they played two exhibition games in the States, one in Salt Lake City and one in San Jose, California, losing both 4–1 before heading overseas in early November. The event was the Three Nations Cup in Mikkeli, Finland. Originally billed as a four nation tournament, the U.S. had rescinded the invitation in the aftermath of the terrorists' attack on September 11. This left Canada, Finland and Sweden to contest the gold medal. Canada won handily, defeating the Finns 5–2 in the final, the victory never in doubt after Hayley Wickenheiser notched the first goal at the eleven-second mark of the opening period. Without the U.S. presence, the Canadians turned the event into an intensive training camp with full practices and off-ice training interspersed among four games in six days. Danièle Sauvageau, in an understatement, said, "It's a lot of hockey and training and travelling in less than six days. It will be good preparation for the Olympic experience."

The Olympic team for Salt Lake City was announced at a press conference at CHA headquarters on Tuesday, November 20. Twenty-one individuals were named including spare goaltender Charline Labonte. Nine would be first-time Olympians. The roster: Dana Antal, Kelly Bechard, Jennifer Botterill, Thérèse Brisson, Cassie Campbell, Isabelle Chartrand, Lori Depuis, Nancy Drolet, Danielle Goyette, Geraldine Heaney, Jayna Hefford, Becky Kellar, Caroline Ouellette, Cheryl Pounder, Tammy Lee Shewchuck, Sami Jo Small, Colleen Sostorics, Kim St-Pierre, Vicky Sunohara and Hayley Wickenheiser. Thirty athletes had been under the microscope since the World's in April. Twenty-one jubilant selectees left Father David Bauer Arena that afternoon. Nine would now put their Olympic dream on hold.

There was little time for the appointed to sit and be smug. The next round of the TSN Challenge Series kicked into gear on November 27 with a game against the States at the Corel Centre in Ottawa. Spurred on by the exhortations of nearly 8,000 nationalistic patrons, the Canadians jumped into a two-goal lead. The euphoria was short-lived, the U.S.A. responding with five unanswered goals. Danièle was blunt in her assessment of the outcome, "We've got a lot of work ahead of us."

Before the game, three veterans were assigned special responsibilities to lead the way to the Olympics. Cassie Campbell, age twenty-eight, was appointed captain. Her two assistants were Hayley Wickenheiser, age twenty-three, and Vicky Sunohara, age thirty-one. All three had received their Olympic baptism at Nagano; they'd stayed the course for four more years and a second chance at the top step on the podium. For Sauvageau, the decision for captain was not lightly taken, but, in the end, an easy one. "Cassie relates well to all the players," she said. "She will be a very positive force in the dressing room and on the ice."

The tide didn't turn for Team Canada in the next two games in the Challenge Series. Once again, they squandered a two-goal lead in Montreal, losing 4–3 despite the rabid urgings of a Quebec crowd cheering for hometown hero Kim St-Pierre, in goal. In Hamilton, a hockey town and a solid supporter of the women's game, the Canadians lost 1–0. The Americans had, for the second time in the year, swept a TSN series.

Sauvageau was philosophical about the outcome: "We only named our team last week. Up to then, the players' goal was individual: to make the team. I'd rather lose eight to the U.S.A. to get that one win at the Olympics we've been working on so hard." Her veteran players agreed with her assessment. Vicky Sunohara added a caveat, "In the big picture, these exhibition games are going to mean nothing, so we won't dwell on them. The important thing is not to lose confidence."

Patience was key. Sauvageau had altered the team's system of play. It would take time for the players to find a new comfort zone. She was willing to sacrifice short-term goals, like winning games, to reach the end goal: gold. The plan could not be slave to a won-lost record.

Just before Christmas, the team travelled east to Newfoundland. Four games were played between December 18 and 22. St. John's, Gander, Corner Brook and Grand Falls opened their arms and their hearts, as only Maritimers can do, to welcome the girls. The Russians were the opposition this time. Their physical play couldn't compensate for the Canadians' skill and they were swept 6–0, 8–1, 8–1 and 6–1. In five short months, from meeting in Calgary to the close of 2001, the Canadian team had crossed a nation from sea to sea.

After Newfoundland, the players were given a week-long hiatus from hockey to return home for the Christmas break. Danièle and Ryan Jankowski, the video expert, had put together a Christmas package for each to open under the tree. It was a video entitled *Just Smile*. The footage documented good times the team had shared together over the 2001 season: the obstacle course at Val Cartier; an aerobic session in the gym; a Finnish sauna experience; a game of foot hockey, a favourite warm-up; gift-giving at the end-of-the-year Christmas party. Sauvageau knew friends and family would question the players on their hockey lives to date, foremost being their record versus the United States. Happiness was a state of mind. The video was her way of saying life was more than just a hockey game.

There were three more dates marked on the Canada versus U.S.A. calendar: January 5 in Chicago, January 6 in Detroit and January 8 in Vancouver. Brash and confident, the States denied Canada victory in all three, beating the Canucks 3–1, 7–4 and 3–2 respectively. The Americans still had an edge to their game that the home side was lacking. Without a doubt, the U.S.A. held bragging rights going into the Olympics.

Sauvageau salvaged a measure of optimism from the Final Face-off game in Vancouver. "We were all over them," she said. "We could have easily won that game. We outplayed them for fifty-five minutes. It was just five minutes that killed us. If we play sixty minutes in Salt Lake, we'll be okay." Although the team had lost on the scoreboard, they had won a psychological battle. They would head into the Olympics believing they could win. Danièle took that ray of sunshine into the last four weeks.

Someone had to pay the price for eight consecutive losses to a strong U.S. side revealing no apparent weaknesses. Sauvageau was the target. The executives at CHA headquarters were growing restless. Like a pit bull on the prowl, the press was sniping hard at her heels. As the pressure mounted, Sauvageau, in classic style, maintained her cool. Asked what was missing in her team, she replied simply: "I guess the belief in getting there as one, as a team. As far as I am concerned, we've been the underdogs for four years. When the puck is dropped in Salt Lake City, the eight games we've played the U.S.A. will be behind both teams."

The annals of sport are sprinkled with a fistful of rivalries for the ages: Ali versus Frazier in the ring, Connors and McEnroe on the courts, Palmer and Nicklaus on the links, Montreal and Toronto in hockey, Green Bay and Dallas on the gridiron. And now, Canada versus the United States in women's ice hockey can be added to this select list of classic confrontations.

Like the bully on the beach, Team Canada kicked sand in the face of its southern neighbour for close to a decade, starting with the first world championship in Ottawa in 1990. For the next three World's, Canada maintained its haughty air. Things changed in 1998 with Nagano and the first Olympics for women's ice hockey. In Japan, for the first time, the underling kicked back, first with a boot to a chin in the preliminaries, the U.S. beating Canada 4–3; then, they delivered a resounding uppercut to the heart and the head in the final by winning 3–1. From that moment forward, the big bully wasn't quite so big anymore.

With the gold medal victory in Nagano, the U.S. women's ice hockey program had secured its place in the sun. Corporate sponsors opened their chequebooks and government funding was set aside in the drive for gold again on American turf in 2002. In short order, the program had cash, cache and a high profile player in Cammi Granato, the team captain and media darling. With cash in the coffers, the notion of bringing the team together to train well before Salt Lake City had become eminently affordable.

In September 2000, the American girls gathered in Lake Placid, New York, under the guidance of Ben Smith. The affable coach had come on board in 1996 to prepare the team for Nagano. A Harvard grad, class of '68, he'd carved a career coaching boys and men at the high school, college and international levels. Prior Olympic experience consisted of a stint with the men's team as an assistant coach at the '88 Winter Games in Calgary. Most of his coaching was done at the college level, with stopovers at Boston University, Dartmouth and a five-year term at Northeastern. His father was a roommate of John F. Kennedy at Harvard and had helped him with his presidential campaign in 1960.

The notion of coaching the women's team in their first Olympics excited him. He joked about working with an elite group of athletes who would finally listen to him. The United States Hockey Association offered him a three-year contract from 1996 through to the end of Nagano. Smith was happy to commit and eager to see where this new path would lead him. He couldn't have dreamed of greater glory. His yellow brick road led him to gold in Nagano with a team that surprised itself and a nation. The chance to continue the journey to Salt Lake City with a shot at a second gold was too enticing for Ben to resist.

The 2001 season had been a watershed one for the Americans. They'd compiled a 31–0 record overall, including 8–0 in their ongoing war against the Canadians. Heading into the Olympics, Smith played his "aw shucks" role to the hilt, astutely dismissing his team's clean-as-a-whistle record against the Canucks. "Playing the Canadians," he'd say after each victory, "was like playing in a mirror. Both sides have equal firepower. Only the bounces make the difference."

CHAPTER 13

Four Weeks to Go

No stone was too small to leave unturned.

BACK IN CALGARY, with four weeks to go before Salt Lake and the 2001 travelling road show finally over for the Canadians, the time had come to fine-tune the run for gold. One imperative over the time remaining was to ensure the players were fully conditioned to play sixty minutes of high-intensity hockey at Salt Lake's elevation. Preparation for the higher altitude had begun back in November 2000 with the Four Nations Cup in Provo, Utah. High volume training at the Val Cartier Camp had built the aerobic base. Much of the remaining time would be devoted to high-intensity training.

The program Danièle initiated in consultation with Dr. Norris worked on several fronts. In the gym on the spinning bicycles and on the ice, the athletes were driven very hard at times. These workouts forced them into a hypoxic, or low oxygen state. Repeated, closely spaced sets of sprints would leave their bodies starved for oxygen at the end. Over time, the training would enhance performance as the athletes' bodies adapted to the demands placed on them.

In another adaptive measure designed to improve the body's efficiency in utilizing oxygen, an oxygen chamber where the oxygen concentration could be artificially regulated was used to simulate low oxygen situations like those experienced at high altitude. No stone was too small to leave unturned.

In November and December, the team had played two games against a mixed squad of junior A and ex-NHL players. Sauvageau added more of these tilts to the hockey schedule in January. The Calgary Royals and the Red Deer Chiefs, two midget triple A teams, happily agreed, despite their hectic schedules, to play Team Canada four more times. Says Sauvageau, "These games brought us to the next level. When you go into the corner with a talented sixteen- or seventeen-year-old hockey player used to hard, physical play, you need to be very strong on the puck. We had to think faster, execute faster and practise our systems under pressure."

The fine-tuning continued on another front. Midway through January, Sauvageau spoke with the team's nutritionist, Kelly Ann Carter-Erdman. A graduate of the nutrition program at the University of Calgary, she had worked with dozens of national teams in a variety of sports over the years. She brought to her profession the perspective of a high-performance athlete, having competed for Canada in cycling in the 1992 Summer Games in Barcelona, Spain. Sauvageau was concerned about the energy level of her players nearing the end of a game. She and the nutritionist agreed to try a revised approach to eating. The athletes were well-versed in the basics of sound nutrition with diets low in fat, high in carbohydrates and bolstered with proteins. Over an eighteen-month period, since the Four Nations Cup in Provo, Erdman had compiled a series of three-day dietary records on each player. The information she gathered went hand-in-hand with the blood work Dr. Norris and Dr. Leclerc, the team physician, were doing. Where iron counts were low, nutritional or pharmaceutical interventions were used to help raise the levels.

The typical pre-game meal for the players—pasta or potato, chicken breasts or steak and a salad—didn't change. What was altered was the length of time before a game that it was eaten.

Throughout the season, players had been eating their big meal, the one that would sustain them through a game, five or six hours ahead of time. Those numbers were reduced. Now, and through the Olympics, they would be sitting down at the dinner table three or four hours ahead of time. Power bars and sport drinks would help maintain their level of energy throughout the game.

For Coach Sauvageau, the focus shifted to another front a scant two weeks before the Games would begin. The decision was one she had agonized over for days. She summoned Nancy Drolet into her office. "I am replacing you at forward," she announced. Her voice was unwavering. And, her conviction. She'd reviewed her decision over and over and now was at peace with herself. She knew she had turned a player's world upside down, but the time had come to inform the athlete and turn the page. As coach of the team, it was her responsibility to lead, to be straightforward and honest, and to do, in the end, what was best for the team.

The press went wild. Wasn't this clearly the hand of a panicked coach now pressing all the wrong buttons, they asked. Nancy Drolet had amassed more points in her career than all but two other players at the national level. Still, 2001 had not gone well for her, her points' production significantly down from previous years. Sauvageau had waited patiently, but the player's game never did come around. Drolet appealed her decision to a committee composed of one representative from the CHA, one from Sport Canada and one from the Players' Association. The appeal committee ruled in Sauvageau's favour. Sherie Piper, a twenty-year-old rookie, was the new player, the one on the hot seat. With her lightning-quick speed off the mark and an edge to her play, Danièle felt she could provide the spark the team so desperately needed. And she knew Piper could take the heat.

The announcement unsettled the team, but less than Danièle had expected. Perhaps it was Sunohara's words, "It could have been any one of us," that affirmed for the players the whimsical nature of fate and, with it, their own vulnerability. They soon settled down to focus on the task at hand.

The last three days before departure, the team headed into the Rockies for one final bout of acclimatization before Salt Lake City. Emerald Lake is a picture-postcard setting in the Rocky Mountains just across the British Columbia border. Physiologically speaking, this was the "unloading phase" in the training program with one environmental stressor, the high altitude, added to further prepare for the physical demands down the road. Time spent here wasn't about on-ice workouts; rather, the focus was on team-building and mental preparation.

In one session headed by Hayley Wickenheiser, a list of "things to expect at the Olympics" was reviewed. Items red-carded for discussion ran the gamut: dealing with the media, playing on the Americans' home turf, listening to the media hype about the powerhouse U.S. team, living in the Village, handling the referee's calls when those calls go against you. There were, at least, a baker's dozen on the list.

The team hit the ice once, on an outdoor rink lined with wooden boards banked by snow and framed by a ring of mountains. It was in the heart of town. The players came equipped for an old-fashioned game of pond shinny with sticks and skates and a hockey puck in hand. Little did they know, however, what lay in store. They started to wonder when Sauvageau summoned Steve Norris, the one who rode them ragged over all those hours on the spinning bikes, to her side. "Are you ready girls?" he began. For the next half hour, he commanded the show: "Up, down, left, right, forward, back." The girls huffed and puffed and soon a crowd of people from town circled the rink, impressed by the athleticism and the red faces. "We had no idea," says Vicky Sunohara, "we'd be doing a fitness workout that day." Dr. Norris had been on-board with Sauvageau since Day One to prepare the players physically for Salt Lake. Her invitation to him to be a part of the retreat at Emerald Lake was really a thank-you note for the work he had done.

Mostly though, Emerald Lake was about relaxing in a beautiful mountain setting, hanging out with teammates and filling the tank for the end of the drive to Olympic gold. It was the final piece in the preparation puzzle. When the team departed for Salt Lake City they would be physically and mentally ready for the challenge ahead.

CHAPTER *14*

The Olympic Games

*The time had finally come to turn dreams
into reality.*

SALT LAKE CITY, Utah, sits smack dab in the middle of an eighty-mile corridor punctuated at its southern end by Provo and at its northern tip by Ogden, and flanked along its length by the imposing Wasatch Front mountain range. The first white settlers to the area arrived long before the Olympics were kindled once again in 1896, inspired by the vision of the Frenchman, Baron Pierre de Coubertin. A tiny band of Mormons, 147-strong led by Brigham Young, arrived in the valley in the summer of 1847. A salt lake stretching northwest into miles of desert inspired the name for the pioneers' new home. Today, the valley cradles most of Utah's 2.2 million people with close to 180,000 calling Salt Lake home. With this number of people, Salt Lake bore the distinction of being the most populous Winter Games site ever. It also marked the first time since 1980 that the games of ice and snow had been hosted by the United States. For the athletes, the most significant figure was the 1,330 metres (4,327 feet) above sea level of their Olympic destination. Not a Mexico City at more than 2,000 metres, but enough elevation to have an impact on performance without proper preparation.

The International Olympic Committee selected Salt Lake, the site of the nineteenth Winter Olympics, years before the

Mom and Dad Sauvageau are happy to be a part of the Olympic crowd in Salt Lake City. (Joanne Ter Harmsel)

Games took place. From the outset, the organizing committee was dogged with controversy related to the bidding process, with the words scandal and bribery hanging like a dark cloud over its head. However, as the count spiralled downward to the start of the Games, the blackness lifted. Once again, the Olympic spirit prevailed. A 900-square-mile stage of mountain and valley was set for the greatest athletic show on earth.

The Canadian women's hockey team boarded a plane from Calgary bound for Salt Lake City on February 6, 2002. Twenty-one players, the top of the pyramid in a country that boasts more than 3,000 times that number playing in leagues from coast to coast, would carry our female hockey hopes into the Games. For these women, solely dedicated to a single purpose, the time had finally come to turn dreams into reality, to show the world, and themselves, they had the right stuff to claim the golden prize.

For ten members of the women's team, Salt Lake would be their first Olympic experience. Eleven sage veterans carried with them lessons learned from Nagano. They had stayed on the top of the hockey heap for four long years in pursuit of their personal grail, Olympic gold, driven to be the best of the best. This time, they refused to be burdened with the weight of a nation's golden expectations, a load that carried over time, they knew, would break even the strongest backs. Best to leave that burden on the Americans to bear, with their sterling 31–0 record for the season and playing on their home turf. Let them feel the insidious pressure of great expectations, the kind that wiggles its way under your skin and into your bones before you even know it's there. Sauvageau had told her team to forget the record, the 0–8. There was strength and character and courage to be drawn from adversity. When the moment arrived, only one game would matter. The game for gold.

Like every Olympics before, and those that will follow, the Games are a heady mix of pomp and ceremony and peak athletic performance. The challenge is to savour the former and attain the latter.

The fanfare and flag waving officially began on February 8 with the Opening Ceremonies. Seventy-eight nations marched into Rice-Eccles Olympic Stadium, the colours of the world in a gaudy parade witnessed by the 50,000 people who filled the stands and the millions more riveted to TV screens around the world. The Salt Lake City Organizing Committee had poured close to $2 billion dollars into the production, making these Games the costliest ever.

The timing was perfect for the hockey women. They could savour the celebration and imbibe the Olympic spirit, knowing the opening match in their quest for the prize was still three days away. Sauvageau remembers the feeling invoked as the

Opening unfolded: "This was the day everybody had been waiting for. Here we were, not Team Hockey but Team Canada. I'll never forget that woman's voice when she announced 'Team Canada' and we walked into the stadium. The ceremony was at night, but it was like day there were so many flashes popping. I had such a feeling of pride for my country.

"I remember standing on the stadium floor thinking this is it. The dream is over. Tomorrow morning, we must get back to our focus. We're not here to compete, we're here to win."

Setting the wheels in motion to win began the next morning with a light workout on the bikes. Over the ensuing two weeks, until the anticipated gold-medal game, there would be an easy mix of on-ice practices, off-ice workouts, games and downtime. "Even though this was the Olympics, nothing was rushed," says Sauvageau. "Even when we practised, it was just to work on the little things. We'd spent two years preparing for this moment. The systems were in place."

An athlete could imbibe the Olympic spirit twenty-four hours of the day, but that wasn't the way of the hockey girls. They were housed, two to a room, in suites of four or eight. On off-days, some were spectators at Olympic events. Many were content just to spend time with family and friends or other athletes from other sports in the Village. Danièle had worked long and hard to get the parents, her staunchest supporters, here. Some of the funds earmarked for the hockey team went to ensuring that they could come. "They deserved a return on their investment," she states matter-of-factly.

Monday, February 11, 2002. West Valley City. Canada versus Kazakhstan. Let the Games begin.

Twenty Canadian women had had this date circled in red on their calendars for a long, long time. The first game on the first day of women's hockey at the 2002 Games was about to begin.

Excitement bubbled in the dressing room as the players laced their skates, readying themselves to step onto the ice at the E-Center in West Valley City. "It seems like it has taken forever," said Sauvageau, thinking about the training and preparation over months and years leading to this moment. The outcome really wasn't in doubt; still, the anticipation, the sense of mission this game brought filled the room. Kazakhstan was a newcomer to the international scene in women's hockey, making its first International Ice Hockey Federation foray at the 2001 World Championships in Minneapolis, where it finished last in the Eight Nation tournament. This would likely mirror its final standing at the Olympics.

The veteran, Wickenheiser, opened the scoring for Canada at 2:33 of the first period on a powerplay. By period's end, the Canucks were up 3–0. The second and third frames were equally one-sided. The final score: Canada 7, Kazakhstan 0. The Kazakhs had been outshot 66–11. Coach Alexander Maltsev of the losing contingent did not despair. "To play Canada is an honour," he said. The Canadian girls were relieved to have their first game completed.

Wednesday, February 13, 2002. Salt Lake City. Canada versus Russia.

Once again, the Canadians went into battle with a comfortable edge in skill and experience over their opponent. Unlike the Russian hockey men who had a long and storied history as warriors on the international stage, the women were new to battle with the 2000 Holiday Tournament in Lake Placid, New York, marking their debut. Competitive hockey for women was still in its infancy in the country's culture of sport. Still, the Russians had worked hard to elevate their game, cementing their status as a nation on the rise by beating Finland 2–1 in the bronze-medal game at the 2001 World's. On this day though, the Ruskies were no match for the hustling Canadians who duplicated their 7–0 score and outshot their opponent 60–6.

Saturday, February 16, 2002. Provo. Canada versus Sweden.

This was Canada's third and final game in its pool. Both teams started on the ground floor in the women's game at the international level with the first World's in Ottawa. Canada had maintained its dominance over Sweden since then. The Swedes crossed the Atlantic twice in 2001 to play the Canadians in exhibition tours. Since international competition began, the blue and yellow had yet to claim a single victory. They were a prime example of a women's team needing an infusion of money and other support from its sports governing body to develop its program. On the ice, in front of a full house, Canada extended the skein of victories, winning handily 11–0 while firing seventy shots at the Swedish goalie. Victory meant the top placing in their pool of four and a date with Finland in the semi-final.

Tuesday, February 19, 2002. West Valley City. Canada versus Finland. Semi-Final.

Since 1990, Finland has tried hard to shed its status as third in line for hockey's throne. In six World Championships and several Nations Cups, it has stood on the third podium step, always surpassed by Canada and the U.S.A. Would these Olympics unveil a different fate?

Canada seemed well on its way to an easy victory, two goals up before the ten-minute mark of the first period. However, the feisty Finns would not be vanquished without a fight. They snapped the shutout with a goal at the end of the first, and added two more early in the second. At the end of the period, their one-goal lead still stood. The Canadians had outplayed and outshot the Finns 40–13 but their tiny goalie, Tuula Puputti, had thwarted their efforts time and again.

Heading into the dressing room between periods, the Canadians found themselves face-to-face with an opponent who didn't roll over early for the first time in the tournament. They stepped on the ice at the start of the third refusing to believe that the game wasn't theirs. They'd faced adversity many times over in 2001. Down a goal in a game they had dominated was but a bump on the road to a win. Wickenheiser potted the equalizer just over three minutes into the third. In the blink of an eye, Hefford followed with another tally.

Sunohara, Campbell and Brisson added three more. In the end, the Canadians, their muscles flexed, outgunned the Finns 7–3. By the time the game ended, little Puputti had been peppered with fifty-four shots. For Sauvageau et al, this hard-fought game was a perfect primer to ride into the final.

CHAPTER *15*

The Gold Medal Game

A golden tear.

SAUVAGEAU woke early on the morning of February 21. She'd slept fitfully through the night, her thoughts never far from the day ahead, the day of the gold-medal game. Kimberley Amirault, the team psychologist, was sharing a room with her in the Olympic village. It was a typical village room with just enough space for two beds, a small desk, a closet and a chest of drawers.

Amirault's was a hectic schedule, up at 5:30 a.m. every day to catch a bus to Soldier's Hollow, an hour's ride away in the mountains, to watch the cross-country ski team perform. She worked with the athletes on this team, too. Early in the afternoon, it was back to Salt Lake to be with the hockey team, at their practices, at their games, incorporating herself into its daily routine. She and Danièle had talked a lot about how this day, the one they'd worked toward for two years now, would unfold. Both had decided it was important to keep the team together and loose. They wanted to go into the game as one, united in purpose, confident and cool. "It's going to be a beautiful day," Danièle announced to Kimberley that morning.

The previous evening, it was agreed the team would gather in a Village conference room for a brief meeting before breakfast. Geraldine Heaney, the "iron woman" of the ice

Finally, the gold-medal game day has arrived.

hockey team, having cemented a position on the national squad without interruption since 1990, had arranged a surprise for the group. She stood at the door waiting to greet her visitors. Jamie Salé and David Pelletier, the now-famous figure skating pair at the centre of a judging scandal, soon appeared. They sauntered into the room, both adorned with their newly received gold medals on ribbons wrapped around their necks. Jamie broke the ice with a warm hello. For the next fifteen minutes, Salé and Pelletier talked about their experiences in skating: handling pressure, relishing the moment, not being afraid to win, skating with passion, believing in yourself and in each other—in short, what it takes to win Olympic gold.

The table of Olympians sat in rapt attention. Pelletier reached forward, his gold medal in hand. He held it tantalizingly close to the faces before him. "You can look, but not touch," he said softly. "It's up to you to win your own." As the two skaters departed, Sauvageau turned and looked at the twenty players who would carry Canada's hopes into the gold-medal game that afternoon. "There are four ways to love," she began, "with your body, mind, heart and soul. Go out today and play with your hearts and souls."

Ryan Jankowski, the team's video specialist, took care of the next item on the agenda that morning. He had put together a series of clips showing each player in action, each profile accompanied by her favourite piece of music. While the video rolled, Sauvageau talked about the role that each of the players, the "real actors," as she often called them, would have in the upcoming game. In a few hours, the curtain would be lifting on the real-life drama with the players performing on a world stage.

At 9:00 a.m., the team assembled for the second time that morning in the Village cafeteria. Breakfast took place with the players, Danièle, Mel, Wally and Karen seated together around a long table, the way an extended family would do at Christmastime. The mood was upbeat. Conversation flowed freely, with lots of chatter, but little focus on the upcoming game. The players had learned from past experience not to narrow their world to a stick and a puck until they were in the dressing room. To start that process now left too much time for nerves to sit on a razor's edge. A better idea was to scrutinize the offerings for the morning meal.

There was, as usual, a bountiful harvest of foods to choose from: bagels and breads, pastries, muffins, pancakes and waffles, hot and cold cereals, eggs, bacon, ham and sausage, and plenty of fresh fruit, yogurt and granola. The food in the Village was a country fair, deli counter, donut shop and diner rolled into one. Athletes could eat twenty-four hours of the day if they wanted.

The time after breakfast was consumed by simple, mundane activities. Danièle returned to her room to read and reflect on the last big push. Others hung out in the lounge, watching events on the Olympic-size screen, playing cards, reading, chatting quietly among themselves or with athletes from other sports.

Mid-morning, the team collected once again to head out into the Salt Lake sunshine for a last walk together as a team. "There was such an energy in the air," Danièle recalls. "The sky was Wedgewood blue and scattered with cotton ball clouds, the kind you want to curl up in. The mountains seemed so close, like I could just reach out and touch them. The players were laughing and chatting away, happy, seemingly without a care in the world. For me, it was a good sign." On the way back to the Village, she spotted some of the American team, also out for a pre-game stroll. "Their heads were down. They were so quiet. It reminded me of us in Nagano. I knew then that this game was ours."

At 2:00 p.m., the team boarded the bus for the thirty-minute ride to the E Center in the downtown core. The game didn't start until 5:00 p.m., Mountain Standard Time, but it was important to plan well in advance. After the September 11 terrorist attacks on the World Trade Center in New York City and the Pentagon in Washington, D.C., security was tight, the tightest ever for an Olympic Games. Close to US$400,000 had been poured into safeguarding the sites. Sixty city, state and national enforcement agencies acted in concert to make this happen. More than 15,000 personnel, including a massive contingent of camouflaged National Guardsmen, patrolled the streets, manned barricades at every venue, checked individual bags, and deployed X-ray machines and handheld magnetometers to ensure the safety of the athletes and the onlookers. Danièle had noted, "Getting around is like travelling to the airport five times in a day."

Every member of the national team party had to wear a photo identification card. As the team members disembarked from the bus, they were whisked through security. First, they were stopped at a barricade, then their bags were checked by a man waving a magnetometer. These measures took a lot of time. Danièle had anticipated disruptions like this long before the team's arrival in Salt Lake. She and Amirault had worked with the team on handling distractions with a minimum of fuss and not expending emotional energy or losing focus on the niggling things.

Two hours before game time, security cleared, the players gathered in their dressing room, an inner sanctum in the sweeping dome off-limits to the outside world. Final preparations would now begin. One of the favourite warm-ups for the players was foot hockey, a loose combination of hockey and soccer. A group of diehards headed into the corridor to set up a game. Others headed to a gleaming chrome set of stationary bicycles. Sauvageau had imported them from Calgary especially for this occasion. The players had ridden countless kilometres on these modified versions of a two-wheeler as part of their training regime. Dr. Norris and the strength and conditioning staff had coaxed and cajoled the team through interminable repeats of bicycle sprints. Sauvageau wanted to bring back the memories: "They'd trained so hard. The bicycles would be a reminder it wasn't for nothing."

Danièle had overhauled the warm-up since Nagano. "Before the final game in 1998," she says, "we had the stopwatches out. Everyone rode. That was mandatory. The coaching staff timed the rides. Thirty seconds on, thirty seconds off. It was too serious." Sauvageau didn't want this Olympic experience to be like that. Why be here if you can't enjoy it? she asked herself. "Life is too short. I wanted the girls to have fun." Foot hockey, bike rides, rope jumping, sprints in the corridor; the warm-up, this time, was the players' choice.

With a half hour to go until game time, the players were dressed. Robin McDonald, the equipment manager, had made things easy for the combatants. He had ordered the equipment at their cubicles the same way he had done it a thousand times before: shin pads in one corner, gloves in another; sweater, pants and shoulder pads hanging from hooks in the stalls. Skates neatly aligned on the floor. Everything was arranged to ensure a minimum of fuss.

Robin was one of a handful of support staff who travelled with the team. They were vital cogs to the team's smooth functioning in the daily training grind over months and years that is part and parcel of getting to the top. These people were now being rewarded with a piece of the action in the game that was the national team's goal all along, the one that counted most.

Doug Stacey was the team trainer, taking care of the bumps and bruises, strains and sprains accumulated along the way. Mavis Wahl was the masseuse soothing the inevitable aching muscles. David Jamieson, the goaltending coach, had played on the men's national team for a year in the eighties. Away from hockey, he taught school. His classroom for the Olympic run had two pupils: Sami Jo Small and Kim St-Pierre. This four-year-old tandem had shared puck-stopping duties since Nagano. Ryan Jankowski stood in the stands, capturing the on-ice action on film for future review. Karen Hughes had accompanied the team to Salt Lake as a third coaching assistant. She would sit in the stands high atop the action relaying her insights to the bench below from a different perspective. Like Wally and Mel, the other assistants, she found little time to imbibe of the Olympics outside hockey. Days for all three were consumed by games, practices and scouting. "Once," says Karen, "Mel and I went to see curling."

Four-thirty p.m. Sauvageau walked out of the coaches' office into the dressing room. Her eyes ran the length of the cubicles. Some of the players were laughing, others talked quietly, some looked straight ahead at a phantom spot on the wall. Others sat, Walkmans on, heads resting in their hands.

Part of the Olympic team staff, left to right: Robin McDonald, Doug Stacey, Dr. Suzanne Leclerc, Wally Kozak, Danièle Sauvageau, Melody Davidson, Kimberley Amirault, Ryan Jankowski (in front).

(Joanne Ter Harmsel)

Everyone had a different way to prepare mentally for the task ahead. Sauvageau looked and listened, quietly gauging the mood of the players. She liked to do this before a game. Today, the room was serene. Danièle had a good feeling about this game.

Four-forty-five p.m. It was time to hit the ice. Sauvageau walked down the cavernous corridor behind the players to the ice. Her assistants, Davidson, Kozak and Hughes, were with her. They had done all they could do. The science was covered, the Xs and Os on the board. The game was the players' responsibility now. Sauvageau had promised herself, almost two years ago, that at the end of the run, she wanted to be at peace with herself. She felt that peace. Now, her intuitive side spoke. She pulled a gold pen from her pocket. On the backside of a tiny bench, raised so the players could access the ice, she wrote the score: Canada 5, U.S.A. 2. Today, more than ever, she would rely on her tactical wizardry and uncanny sixth sense behind the bench. Was her premonition right? Only time would tell.

The Americans should have swaggered onto the ice surface at the E Center for the opening face-off like Wyatt Earp riding into town at high noon to shoot down the bad guy at fifty paces. After all, Utah was the perfect Wild West setting. Plus, the Americans boasted a perfect record, now 34–0 including 8–0 against the Canucks coming into this showdown. They had plenty of ammunition to support a swagger. But they didn't.

From the opening face-off, they seemed unsure. Wickenheiser swore she could see the fear in their eyes. She must have been right. The Canadians delivered the opening salvo. Cherie Piper did the job she had been brought on board to do. Darting like a whirligig after the puck, she chased it down behind the net and tried a wrap-around. Her big right winger, Caroline Ouellette, parked near the crease like a big Mack truck, walloped the rebound home. The bench erupted. When the whole world doubted after those eight losses, these players looked to themselves for strength and support. For Sauvageau, the goal was a golden moment. The boot camp at Val Cartier, centralization, the 0 and 8, she wanted so much for these girls to take responsibility, to take their place, to play as one.

Midway through the first period, the whistle of Stacey Livingstone, the American referee, took over. The penalties mounted. Through the rest of the first and into the second, there were eight in a row to the Canadian team. Sauvageau set the tone. She didn't waver, didn't even blink. Her police experiences had taught her well: "I couldn't change the situation, so I just had to make the best of it. The game was not about the ref, not about the U.S.A., it was all about us." The girls on the bench followed her steadfast lead. Fine, they decreed, if we have to play the Americans four on five, that's what we'll do.

117

When the buzzer sounded to end the first period, the players filed into the dressing room. Seated together away from the enemy and the prying eyes of the world, their guard slipped. The stoic demeanour and firm resolve they exhibited so admirably out on the ice started to crumble. The ref's whistle still shrilled in some ears as cries of "foul" and "unfair" bounced off the walls of the room. "Emerald Lake," said Dana Antal, a soft-spoken rookie in her first Olympics, her voice lifting above the din. Stillness descended on the room, like a morning mist on a wild northern lake. Emerald Lake was a reminder of a place in time, serene and fetching, a fairytale land beyond discord. Sauvageau remembers the moment: "I walked into the room, and the first thing I heard were those words. Emerald Lake was a reminder that, no matter the outcome, we had had a beautiful journey." The players rose as one to return to the ice for the start of the second, at peace with themselves.

Early in the second, the Americans countered on a powerplay. The Canucks remained implacable. Not long after, Wickenheiser, the one with a will of iron, rammed a rebound collected inside the enemy blue line into the twine. Canada 2, U.S.A. 1. She'd accused the Americans of placing the Maple Leaf flag on the floor of the dressing room to spur themselves on. "That'll teach 'em," she later said.

The Canadians' third goal surprised everyone in the rink and around the world. The countdown had started to end the period. There were a scant thirteen seconds left on the clock. Sunohara, centring a line with Lori Dupuis and Jayna Hefford, won the face-off in her end the same way she had done a million times before. This was the sign for Hefford to start moving up the ice. She slipped behind the defence, corralled a one-hundred-foot pass and floated a shot over the flailing pad of the American goalie with a second to go. She was ecstatic: "I knew I didn't have much time, but a second left on the clock, that was unbelievable. Vicky wins so many face-offs. Once I saw we had control, I put my head down and started skating. It was a perfect pass from Becky. DeCosta, the goalie, tried to poke the puck and that's when I put it up and over. I tried not to get too excited. I wanted to stay focused. After all, we still had a period to go."

In the dressing room between periods, the mood had changed. The game was reduced to twenty minutes of hockey now. The players were intent on finishing the business at hand: winning gold. They would take this approach into the third period.

The start of the third period and 1,200 seconds left to Olympic gold. For Sauvageau and eleven veteran players, four years of waiting for another chance—a second chance—was distilled to these twenty minutes of pressure-packed hockey. The last six months had tested Sauvageau's mettle. As the losses mounted to the Americans and the sniping started with a press and public losing faith, Sauvageau stayed the course. She was the calm epicentre in a swirling sea of doubt, always steadfastly believing in herself and her plan, in her team and in the experts who helped shape her vision now unfolding out on the ice. She always found the silver lining: "By having people not believing in us, I think that's when we started believing in ourselves."

Games are won and lost in a heartbeat. The Americans, as proud and as passionate as their Canadian counterparts, had also devoted themselves to this Olympic endeavour. They'd put in their years, honed their bodies and their minds to reach the pinnacle. They wouldn't go quietly into the Utah night.

With 16:27 gone in the third, Karyn Bye slipped a shot from the blue line past St-Pierre in the Canadian goal. Once again, the Americans had found the advantage in a powerplay. Still, Sauvageau didn't flinch. Nor did her players. It takes courage and determination to reach your grail, to look in the eye of victory, wanting it so much, and not be afraid. Here were two teams at the top of their game, at the top of the world.

Four minutes to go with a one-goal lead is an eternity in hockey. Nevertheless, on this Olympic evening, the final one for women's hockey, the Canadian girls would remain steadfast and strong. Time ticked down. Just over a minute to go. The American goalie looked at her coach to get the signal. Ben Smith raised his hand. DeSilva dropped her head, dug her skates into the ice and made a beeline for the bench.

Sauvageau had practised this scenario a thousand times over in the last four weeks: the clock running down, the goalie pulled for an extra attacker. She was prepared, and so was her team. The players she wanted were out on the ice. For fifty-nine minutes, they'd said with their actions on the ice, "This game is ours." They'd accepted responsibility for themselves and each other. They'd played as one to be a champion. They wouldn't let their coach and themselves down now. The final buzzer sounded.

The Canadian Women's Ice Hockey Team was Olympic Champion, the best in the world. Sauvageau flung her arms heavenward. In the stands, her parents embraced.

There are no rehearsals for a gold-medal moment, no practices. The only preparation is the vision in your head of that magic moment that plays itself over and over again. But that is a dream. This was reality. Sauvageau turned to hug her assistants, Melody and Wally and Karen. Together, they'd worked on a plan, coaxed and cajoled twenty proud athletes for just this moment. The players wove through tight little circles on the ice, some giggling like twelve-year-olds on the playground, others hugging, crying, waving or wearing the Canadian flag. Sauvageau stepped off the bench onto the ice to join her flock. She moved among her players, embracing some, sharing words and smiles with others. Then, she summoned her flock to the centre of the ice. They gathered in a circle, twenty hockey players dressed in white, their sweaters crested with a red and black maple leaf. "I am so proud of you," Sauvageau began. She finished her speech with three hallmark words that will always be the stamp of this team: Determination. Courage. Responsibility. A nation, privy to this private moment, will remember these words.

Then came the moment Sauvageau and her stalwart veterans had waited for over four long years. The two hockey teams lined up on the blue line, and the Canadian anthem began to play. The Canadian flag rose slowly toward the E Center ceiling. Danièle's father, high in the stands, gazed up at the big screen overhead. His eye caught a tear running down his daughter's cheek. He stood and watched the teardrop fall. It seemed to stretch all the way to the ice. It wasn't often he'd seen his daughter cry. But, this tear was different. It was a golden tear.

As the dignitaries passed down the line placing gold medals in turn over each player's head, Sauvageau looked skyward. The flags of three countries flew overhead: Canada, the United States, Sweden. Finally, the order was right.

Finally, the order was right.

(Joanne Ter Harmsel)

CHAPTER 16

The End of the Olympic Experience

"Let's just walk on a cloud for a while."

— Danièle Sauvageau

ONE LAST TIME, the girls gathered at the E Center. It was a Sunday afternoon, close to 1:00 p.m. The last day, and the last Olympic event was set to begin. Men's hockey: Canada versus the U.S.A.

The girls were there to return the support the Canadian men had given them. In their final game, Gretzky, Lemieux, et al stood in the stands awed by the iron will of the Canadian girls on the ice below. Wayne Gretzky admitted that their gutsy victory in the face of adversity put added pressure on the men to perform. Pat Quinn called the team's performance the most disciplined effort he had ever seen. Some of the magic must have rubbed off. The men sailed to victory with an inspired effort, winning 5–2. This was the first hockey gold in fifty years for the Canadian men. The Edmonton Mercurys in 1952 in Oslo, Norway, were the last team to stand atop the podium. For the second time in these Olympics, a nation embraced its hockey heroes. In cities and towns across the country, fans streamed out of houses and taverns into the streets, waving flags, honking horns and partying long into the night. In war-torn Afghanistan, our military personnel lay down their rifles to watch the game, fed by satellite to the desert. Even the prime minister, Jean Chrétien, got into the act: "In two golden weeks of triumph, the game we have always called our own, that we have shared with the world, has become ours again." Canada now stood on the summit, the king and queen of the hockey world.

Two Quebec hockey stars stand together, Mario Lemieux and Danièle Sauvageau. (CHA Archives)

The Olympic Games were rapidly drawing to an end. The Closing Ceremonies were back in Rice-Eccles Stadium, where the Games had begun. Once again, the athletes paraded before the world. Seventeen days. Seventy-eight nations. Twenty-five hundred athletes. Two hundred and thirty-four medals. Seventeen for Canada, including two hockey golds. The closing was a collage of colours, music and harmony. The three-hour party was a celebration of human performance and the Olympic spirit. There was music and dance, and 780 children in Eskimo parkas singing jubilantly "Happy Trails to You" from the stadium floor. Huge white beach balls, like giant round snowflakes, floated down from the stands; helium balloons with gyrating gymnasts as skiers and snowboarders soared overhead. Dr. Jacques Rogge, President of the International Olympic Committee, delivered his closing remarks. Unlike his predecessor, Juan Antonio Samaranch, Rogge stayed in the Athletes' Village to be closer to the pulse of the Olympic Games.

The grand theatre on a world stage culminated with a fireworks extravaganza, exploding streaks of green, yellow, red and orange, lighting the sky from eleven sites up and down the valley. The crowning moment came when two little girls, wrapped in parkas, met on the ice of the stadium floor. The Olympic torch was passed from one to the other, and then they skated off into the night. Turin, Italy, would await the flame's arrival four years hence.

For the hockey girls, twenty gold medals wrapped around their necks, taking their final bows, the feeling was one of euphoria, a sense of pride and accomplishment, a feeling of peace in a job well done. Little did they know, cocooned as they were in their Olympic world, that their gold medal performance had captured a nation's heart. On television back home, close to seven million people had cheered them on, riding an emotional see-saw over sixty minutes of heart-stopping action. In a game where the opponents were so evenly matched and the referee's calls one-sided and questionable at best, the team's grit and courage and determination galvanized a country in a way reminiscent of another iconic event in Canadian hockey history: Paul Henderson's famous goal in the 1972 Summit Series, Canada versus the Soviet Union. The girls' win had triggered an emotional outpouring beyond all imagining. They went into the final as the indisputable underdog given little, if any, chance to succeed by a press and a public who'd lost faith long ago with their 0–8 record against the U.S.A.

Credit must go to a coach who always believed this was a journey. "When you climb a mountain, it's not just about getting to the top. It's what's in between that counts for a lot. It's an ongoing process," she would say. "We didn't win because of a single player or person. In the end, we believed in ourselves and in each other and we played as one. That was my ultimate goal."

When the curtain fell on the nineteenth Olympic Games, many of the Canadian athletes returned to Calgary, where they met several hundred who had come out to the airport to deliver a warm and robust welcome to their heroes. The loudest cheer of all was saved for the hockey girls. Theirs was a triumph for the ages. The veterans, especially, savoured this moment. For Geraldine Heaney, the gold medal game was her one hundred and twenty-fifth for the national team and the last one she would play for her country. There was no better way to end a journey.

Danièle Sauvageau was filled with pride, pride for her team and pride for her country. In one exuberant moment she proclaimed if she were a parent she'd be happy to have any and all of her players as her daughters. She felt privileged to coach this team. Her girls were role models nonpareil, not just for girls and women, but for humankind.

In late March, an event was held on Parliament Hill to honour the Olympians. Once again, women's hockey received the loudest and longest ovation of all from the thousands who'd gathered under the Peace Tower to celebrate athletic

Danièle is greeted by her niece, Melissa, and cousin, Samuel, at the airport in Montreal after victory in Salt Lake City.

excellence. The team's spirit and courage through every adversity had become a nation's touchstone, symbolizing the Olympic ideals. After two years of focused effort, Sauvageau was content to ride the wave of Olympic glory: "I think it's important to take the time and enjoy it. A moment like that doesn't happen often, if ever, in your lifetime. Going back too soon into a businesslike approach . . . we've done it, now what? No, let's just walk on a cloud for a while."

CHAPTER 17

Grace Under Pressure

"I believe each of us has a destiny."

— Danièle Sauvageau

A WORLD CONFERENCE on Women and Sport was held in Montreal from May 16 to 19, 2002. More than five hundred delegates representing seventy countries around the globe attended this event. Danièle Sauvageau was in attendance. She had been invited as the distinguished recipient of the Grace Under Pressure Award, an honour bestowed to a select few over the years.

The Canadian Association for the Advancement of Women in Sport is the body behind the award's existence. The organization was founded in 1981 as a joint initiative with Sport Canada, with the impetus to encourage and promote female participation in sport from the grassroots to the Olympic level. In 1986, the association established the Breakthrough Awards to recognize those women who had extended the boundaries for women in sport, either through exceptional athletic performance or as agents of change.

The Grace Under Pressure Award was introduced specifically to celebrate achievement under exceptional circumstances. Silken Laumann, the brightest star in the rowing firmament in the late 1980s and early 1990s, was bestowed the honour in 1997. In her acceptance speech, she conveyed the value of participation in sport for her: "The words, grace under pressure, really tie in with my philosophy of sport, that winning isn't everything, that the pursuit of excellence is what's most important. . . . This award is really special because it acknowledges more than winning. We all win when we pursue our own potential, when we become the best we can be as human beings."

Danièle's journey to a gold medal victory at Salt Lake exhibited all of the qualities the award celebrated, especially including outstanding achievement under exceptional duress. For the vast majority of people watching the final game unfold, captivated by the gritty performance of a Canadian team and its ice-cool leader over sixty minutes, the pressures endured by the players and coach were unfathomable. Even if the strains were enormous, Sauvageau, the orchestrator of this epic victory, was not one to reveal their effect. Behind the bench on this golden night, she appeared unflappable. Only a golden tear as the anthem played hinted at the immense relief this victory had brought.

With the win, Sauvageau became the only female in hockey's overwhelmingly male domain to be a head coach and an Olympic gold medalist. With each American victory in the series leading up to the Olympic Games, she was judged quickly and harshly by her critics. Sauvageau always responded with dignity and poise, always elected to take the high road. She had a mission; she was determined to prevail. It was vital to her to show the world that a woman could succeed in a role traditionally assumed by a man, that coaching was a woman's game too. Responsibility. Courage. Determination. She personified each quality in equal measure, plus a fourth—grace. These four hallmarks of character were her sources of strength along the way. Her professionalism, never once tarnished, will be her legacy.

Since the Olympics, Danièle's life has been a swirling vortex of public appearances. More time is spent in airports and on airplanes travelling to and from public engagements than at her home in Montreal. She's yo-yoed across the country from

St. John's to Vancouver and touched down in countless towns and cities in between. It's not just hockey people who clamour for her services. The agenda includes all sorts of organizations and corporations. She spent a week in Spain sharing her coaching philosophy with the Spanish Sports Federation. Japanese hockey people want her expertise. She's hobnobbed with Prime Minister Jean Chrétien and former U.S. President Bill Clinton. Deux-Montagnes, where she grew up, feted her one day in the spring. The recognition factor is high, particularly in Quebec where she is regarded as a hero. Rarely does she walk down the street without being flagged down by an autograph seeker. Danièle tells the story about an encounter at the airport in Montreal. "I am at the ticket counter. I hear 'Hi, Danièle.' I don't recognize the voice. I'm wondering if it is a friend, a media type, a hockey associate. I turned around.

Danièle is awarded the citizenship medal by the mayor of Deux-Montagnes, Benoît Forget. April 2002. (SPVM Archives)

Michel Sarazin, Montreal city police chief, presents Danièle with a framed picture that now commands an honoured place on the builders' wall at police headquarters. Police reception, March 26, 2002.

(SPVM Archives)

Big media names at the police reception include, left to right: Rejean Tremblay, columnist, *La Presse*; Danièle Sauvageau; Bertrand Raymond, columnist, *Journal de Montréal*; Claude Mailhot, Reseau des Sports; Maxim Roy, actor in tele-series, *Lance et Compte*; Marc Lachapelle, journalist, *Journal de Montréal*.

(SPVM Archives)

This man is walking toward me. He introduces himself. It turns out that we trained together at the RCMP Depot in Regina back in the eighties. We even played a game of hockey together at The Depot. He's followed my career. He talks about the gold-medal game and the impact it had. He says his mom still talks about that game."

Sauvageau has lots to ponder regarding her future. There is her policing career with the Montreal Urban Community Police Service. There are media opportunities on radio and television. The CBC has hired her as a between-periods analyst on the French telecasts of *Hockey Night In Canada*. Once again, she's a trailblazer, the first woman ever to hold this position. She will be appearing for HNIC on the English network intermittently over the season on their special Saturday triple-headers where hockey afficionados can get their fix from mid-afternoon until late into the evening. Outside of hockey, she's been offered marketing positions, public relations work and team-building roles in the financial sector.

Danièle's appointment as coach with the national team ended on June 1, 2002. Early in July, the CHA discussed potential job opportunities in hockey with her over the next couple of years. Danièle decided against a move back to Calgary. She says, "For four years, I've lived in Calgary to coach the national team. I won't do that anymore. Montreal is my home. My family lives here, my friends are here. I'm forty now. I have to start thinking about the quality of my life. The players won't be centralized anyway. Many of them don't live in Calgary. Sometimes, I call myself the Internet coach because of the time I spend on my computer sending e-mails to coaches across the country. I think I could do the same out of Montreal. Still, I've been with the national program for eight years now. I'm prepared to help the women's program at any time. The people in Calgary know I'm just a phone call away."

For more than a decade, Danièle has devoted herself to hockey. The constant travel, eighty-hour work weeks and intense pressure do not form the bedrock of lasting relationships. The time has come to rethink her priorities. "I've spent a long time climbing that mountain to reach hockey's pinnacle," she says. "Do I want to climb that mountain again and again?" Unfortunately, unlike a hockey player who is retired by age forty, she's just coming into her prime as a coach. "I know so much now," she sighs.

Challenge is the engine that drives Danièle. "How best can I use my talents?" she asks. That is the question she must now answer. The opportunities are falling like raindrops from the sky. The notion of sifting through the choices does not daunt her. "It might seem difficult now, but everything will fall into place. I believe each of us has a destiny."

Fortunately, Danièle will still have an impact on the coaching scene. In another serendipitous moment in her life, Danièle becomes the pioneer yet again. The Canadian Coaching Association has asked her to be its spokesperson. It's a new position, created just for her. She will travel the country yet again meeting with and speaking on behalf of coaches in every sport and at every level. "I don't know why they asked me, but I am honoured. This means a lot to me. I've worked so hard to promote coaching and women in coaching. It will be a good transition for me at the end of my hockey career."

One of her goals has always been to make coaching a recognized profession for women. "It's still very much a man's world out there," she says. She relates an anecdote to illustrate her point. "I was at my brother's one evening for a dinner party. Six of us were sitting around the table. My brother is a lawyer. One man at the table was a doctor, another a dentist, another an accountant. We were talking about coaching. Each one, in turn, called himself a coach because that's what he did on a Saturday morning. It made me laugh. I don't say that I am a doctor because I take a first aid course. I'm just not sure that people take coaching seriously as a profession, especially for women."

Will there ever be a woman coach in the National Hockey League? George Gross, a sportswriter for the *Toronto Sun*, believes that day will come and that woman will be Danièle Sauvageau. In an article he wrote for his newspaper, he put the question to Ken Dryden, President of the Toronto Maple Leafs. Dryden was quoted as saying, "I can see a day when a woman could be an assistant coach in the NHL. Then, when a certain confidence and trust developed, she could be promoted." He commended Sauvageau on her poise and control throughout the team's Olympic run and on her speech after the gold-medal game: "It was a speech any male coach would have been proud to deliver. She obviously has what it takes to coach."

As for now, the image of the calm and thoughtful coach guiding her flock through sixty minutes of turbocharged hockey will remain forever emblazoned on a nation's psyche. The spirit of twenty-one individuals who believed in themselves and in each other will never die.

In the warm afterglow of an Olympic victory, the challenge becomes finding the next mountain to climb. Danièle's pioneering spirit will lead her to new places, new people, new experiences, but the team who travelled with her on her Olympic journey will walk with her in spirit forever.

The journey to Olympic glory was not an easy one. There were many who doubted along the way. When they questioned, Danièle responded with grace and dignity. In one golden moment, she and her team transformed a country into a nation of believers. Whatever the mountains she chooses to climb, responsibility, determination, courage and grace under pressure will guide her footsteps along the way.

march 3 02

Dear Danièle,

I 'am very proud that the Canadian hockey teams brought the gold medal home to Canada where they belong. I was sad to learn that as a choach, you did not receive a medal for your contribution to our Canadian woman's team. I won this medal playing hockey and I want you to have it. I am proud of it and I hope you will be too.

Your friend

Meaghan Mahon

#8
westwood warriors
calgary alberta

Meaghon Mahon, a ten-year-old hockey player with the Westwood Warriors in Calgary, offers Danièle the medal she won playing hockey. Coaches do not receive Olympic medals, only athletes.

Appendix 1

Canadian Hockey Association

3M National Coaching Certification Program (NCCP)

1. **Coach**
    - Practical 1
    - Technical 1

2. **Intermediate**
    - Theory 1
    - Practical 2
    - Technical 2

3. **Advanced 1**
    - Theory 2
    - Practical 3
    - Technical 3

4. **Theory 3**

5. **Advanced 2**

6. **Level 4**

7. **Level 5**

Level 4/5 Tasks

1 Energy System

2 Strength Training for Elite Athletes

3 Sport-Specific Performance Factors

4 Nutrition for Optimal Performance

5 Environmental Factors and Performance

6 Recovery and Regeneration

7 Psychological Preparation for Coaches

8 Psychological Preparation for Elite Athletes

9 Practical Coaching: Skill Training

10 Biomechanical Analysis of Advanced Skills

11 Practical Coaching: Strategy & Tactics

12 Planning & Periodization

13 Analyzing Performance Factors

14 Practical Coaching: Training Camps

15 Practical Coaching: Competitive Tour

16 Athlete Long-Term Development

17 Leadership and Ethics

18 Individual Studies

19 Canadian Sport System

20 National Team Program

Appendix 2

Centralization Roster

#	Player	Position	Height	Weight	Birthdate	Hometown	2001 Team	
1	Sami Jo Small	G	5'07	187	03/25/76	Winnipeg, MB	Brampton Thunder, ON	
32	Charline Labonte	G	5'08	150	10/15/82	Boisbriand, QC	Mistral de Laval, QC	
33	Kim St-Pierre	G	5'08	150	12/14/78	Chateauguay, QC	McGill Univ. (CIAU)	
4	Becky Kellar	D	5'07	150	01/01/75	Hagersville, ON	Beatrice Aeros, ON	
5	Colleen Sostorics	D	5'04	174	12/17/79	Kennedy, SK	Oval X-Treme, AB	
6	Therese Brisson	D	5'07	150	10/05/66	Dollard-des-Ormeaux, QC	Mississauga Ice Bears, ON	
11	Cheryl Pounder	D	5'06	145	06/21/76	Mississauga, ON	Beatrice Aeros, ON	
73	Isabelle Chartrand	D	5'05	130	04/20/78	Anjou, QC	St. Lawrence Univ. (ECAC)	Olympic Roster
91	Geraldine Heaney	D	5'08	140	10/01/67	Weston, ON	Beatrice Aeros, ON	
7	Cherie Piper	F	5'05	165	06/29/81	Scarborough, ON	Beatrice Aeros, ON	
12	Lori Dupuis	F	5'08	165	11/14/72	Cornwall, ON	Brampton Thunder, ON	
13	Caroline Ouellette	F	5'11	172	05/25/79	Montreal, QC	Wingstar de Montreal, QC	
15	Danielle Goyette	F	5'07	148	01/30/66	St-Nazaire, QC	Oval X-Treme, AB	
16	Jayna Hefford	F	5'05	140	05/14/77	Kingston, ON	Brampton Thunder, ON	
17	Jennifer Botterill	F	5'09	155	05/01/79	Winnipeg, MB	Harvard Univ. (ECAC)	
22	Hayley Wickenheiser	F	5'09	170	12/08/78	Shaunavon, SK	Oval X-Treme, AB	
23	Dana Antal	F	5'07	135	04/19/77	Esterhazy, SK	Oval X-Treme, AB	
24	Kelly Bechard	F	5'09	145	01/22/78	Sedley, SK	Oval X-Treme, AB	
25	Tammy Lee Shewchuk	F	5'04	138	12/31/77	St-Laurent, QC	Harvard Univ. (ECAC)	
61	Vicky Sunohara	F	5'08	170	11/22/73	Brampton, ON	Oval X-Treme, AB	
77	Cassie Campbell	F	5'07	141	05/18/70	Scarborough, ON	Brampton Thunder, ON	
35	Danielle Dube	G	5'08	145	03/10/76	Vancouver, BC	Richmond, BC	
20	Correne Bredin	D	5'11	190	02/11/80	Warburg, AB	Dartmouth Coll (ECAC)	
34	Delaney Collins	D	5'03	135	05/02/77	Pilot Mound, MB	Oval X-Treme, AB	
44	Fiona Smith	D	5'02	125	10/31/73	Edam, SK	Edmonton Chimos, AB	
72	Nathalie Rivard	D	5'08	160	01/21/72	Cumberland, ON	Mississauga Ice Bears, ON	
10	Gillian Apps	F	5'11	173	11/02/83	Unionville, ON	Beatrice Aeros, ON	
18	Nancy Drolet	F	5'06	145	08/02/73	Drummondville, QC	Vancouver Griffins, BC	
26	Gina Kingsbury	F	5'07	138	11/26/81	Rouyn-Noranda, QC	St. Lawrence Univ. (ECAC)	
39	Amanda Benoit-Wark	F	5'03	135	01/22/76	Welland, ON	Beatrice Aeros, ON	

Appendix 3

International Experience

#	Player	Position	Nagano	1998 3-Nations Cup	1999 World's	1999 4-Nations Cup	2000 World's	2000 4-Nations Cup	2001 World's	Salt Lake City
1	Sami Jo Small	G	x	x	x		x		x	x
32	Charline Labonte	G								x
33	Kim St-Pierre	G		x	x	x	x	x	x	x
4	Becky Kellar	D	x	x	x	x	x	x	x	x
5	Colleen Sostorics	D							x	x
6	Therese Brisson	D	x	x	x	x	x	x	x	x
11	Cheryl Pounder	D		x	x	x	x		x	x
73	Isabelle Chartrand	D				x		x	x	x
91	Geraldine Heaney	D	x	x	x		x	x	x	x
7	Cherie Piper	F								x
12	Lori Dupuis	F	x	x	x		x	x		x
13	Caroline Ouellette	F			x	x	x		x	x
15	Danielle Goyette	F	x	x	x	x	x	x	x	x
16	Jayna Hefford	F	x	x	x	x	x	x	x	x
17	Jennifer Botterill	F	x		x	x	x	x	x	x
22	Hayley Wickenheiser	F	x		x	x	x	x		x
23	Dana Antal	F				x			x	x
24	Kelly Bechard	F				x	x	x	x	x
25	Tammy Lee Shewchuk	F				x	x	x	x	x
61	Vicky Sunohara	F	x	x	x		x	x	x	x
77	Cassie Campbell	F	x	x	x	x	x	x	x	x
35	Danielle Dube	G								
20	Correne Bredin	D							x	
34	Delaney Collins	D					x	x		
44	Fiona Smith	D	x	x	x	x		x		
72	Nathalie Rivard	D		x	x	x	x	x		
10	Gillian Apps	F								
18	Nancy Drolet	F	x	x	x	x	x		x	
26	Gina Kingsbury	F							x	
39	Amanda Benoit-Wark	F		x	x		x	x		

Appendix 4

2000 - 2001 - 2002 Seasons

2000 4-Nations Cup, Provo, Utah
November 6–11, 2000

Round Robin

CAN	9	SWE	0
USA	4	CAN	1
CAN	8	FIN	2

Final

CAN	2	USA	0

2001 January Tour versus Sweden
January 22–29, 2001

Mon. Jan 22	Hanna, AB	CAN 4	SWE 0
Wed. Jan 24	Cranbrook, BC	CAN 8	SWE 0
Thurs. Jan 25	Trail, BC	CAN 8	SWE 0
Sat. Jan 27	Kelowna, BC	CAN 4	SWE 1
Mon. Jan 29	Golden, BC	CAN 9	SWE 2

2001 TSN Challenge Series

Wed. Jan 31	Red Deer, AB	USA 5	CAN 4
Fri. Feb 2	Denver, CO	USA 3	CAN 2

2001 Women's World Hockey Championships, Minneapolis, Minnesota
April 2–8, 2001

Round Robin

CAN	11	KAZ	0
CAN	5	RUS	1
CAN	13	SWE	0

Semifinal

CAN	8	FIN	0

Final

CAN	3	USA	2

2001 October Tour versus Sweden
October 3–6, 2001

Wed. Oct 3	Victoria, BC	**CAN 10**	SWE 0
Fri. Oct 5	Campbell River, BC	**CAN 7**	SWE 0
Sat. Oct 6	Port Alberni, BC	**CAN 10**	SWE 0

2001 Canada versus United States

Sat. Oct. 20	Salt Lake City, Utah	**USA 4**	CAN 1
Sun. Oct 21	San Jose, California	**USA 4**	CAN 1

2001 3-Nations Cup, Mikkeli, Finland
November 2–6, 2001

Round Robin

CAN	5	SWE	0
CAN	7	FIN	4
CAN	5	SWE	1

Final

CAN	5	FIN	2

2001 TSN Challenge Series (Canada versus USA)

Tues. Nov 27	Ottawa, ON	**USA 5**	CAN 2
Wed. Nov 28	Montreal, QC	**USA 4**	CAN 3
Fri. Nov 30	Hamilton, ON	**USA 1**	CAN 0

2001 December Tour versus Russia
Dec 18–22, 2001

Tues. Dec 18	St. John's, NF	**CAN 6**	RUS 0
Wed. Dec 19	Gander, NF	**CAN 8**	RUS 1
Fri. Dec 21	Cornerbrook, NF	**CAN 8**	RUS 1
Sat. Dec 22	Grand Falls, NF	**CAN 6**	RUS 1

2002 Canada versus USA

Sat. Jan 5	Chicago, IL	**USA 3**	CAN 1
Sun. Jan 6	Detroit, MI	**USA 7**	CAN 3
Tues. Jan 8	Vancouver, BC	**USA 3**	CAN 2

Olympic Games Summary
Salt Lake City, Feb. 8–24, 2002

Mon. Feb 11	**Canada**	7	Kazakhstan	0
Wed. Feb 13	**Canada**	7	Russia	0
Sat. Feb 16	**Canada**	11	Sweden	0

Semifinal

Tues. Feb 19	**Canada**	7	Finland	3

Gold Medal Game

Thurs. Feb 21	**Canada**	3	USA	2

Appendix 5

Gold Medal Game Summary

First Period   1. CAN, Ouellette 2 (Piper) 1:45

Penalties   Looney, USA (holding) 6:17
Kennedy, USA (roughing) 10:54
Botterill, CAN (tripping) 12:15
Wickenheiser, CAN (delay of game) 14:05
Brisson, CAN (roughing) 17:01
Sunohara, CAN (cross-checking) 17:52

Second Period 2. USA, King 4 (Granato, Mounsey) 1:59 (pp)
3. CAN, Wickenheiser 7 (Goyette) 4:10
4. CAN, Hefford 3 (Kellar, Brisson) 19:59

Penalties   Kellar, CAN (tripping) 1:11
Ouellette, CAN (roughing) 4:51
Chartrand, CAN (tripping) 11:25
Botterill, CAN (tripping) 14:03
Wendell, USA (charging) 15:37
Ouellette, CAN (holding), Kennedy USA, (roughing) 18:05

Third Period 5. USA, Bye 3 (Mounsey, Potter) 16:27 (pp)

Penalties   Wall, USA (roughing) 0:44
Kellar, CAN (roughing) 1:49
Sostorics CAN (body checking) 5:02
Baker, USA (holding stick), Dupuis, CAN (high sticking) 10:56
Bechard, CAN (tripping) 16:04

Shots on goal	Canada 29	USA 27
Goal	Canada: Kim St. Pierre (W, 4–0)	USA: Sara DeCosta (L, 2–1)
Power-Plays	Goal Chances : Canada 0–4	USA 2–11

Appendix 6

Canadian Player Scoring Statistics

Olympics 2002

	Goals	Assists	Points
Wickenheiser	7	3	10
Goyette	3	7	10
Hefford	3	4	7
Sunohara	4	2	6
Botterill	3	3	6
Ouellette	2	4	6
Piper	3	2	5
Brisson	2	3	5
Antal	2	1	3
Campbell	2	1	3
Chartrand	2	1	3
Dupuis	1	1	2
Shewchuk	1	1	2
Heaney	0	2	2
Sostorics	0	2	2
Bechard	0	1	1
Kellar	0	1	1
St. Pierre	0	1	1

Appendix 7

Distinctions

+ *1995 Head coach of team Quebec – nominated team of the year* : Quebec Sports Awards

+ *1996 Coach of the year*: city of St-Eustache, Quebec

+ *1997–98 Personality of the year*: city of St-Eustache, Quebec

+ *1998 Silver medallist at the Olympic Games* in Nagano, Japan

+ *1999 Named coach of the month for March in Canada*: National Coaching Institute

+ *1999 Person of the year*: Sunday, March 21st *(La Presse)*

+ *1999 Silver medallist World Championships* in Finland

+ *1999 Person of the year*: category «*Social Implication* » **Montreal Urban Police Gala** Excellence

+ *1999 Nominated coach of the year in Canada*: Canadian Coaches Association

+ *2000 Nominated coach of the year*: Quebec Sports Awards

+ *2000 Nominated woman of the year*: YMCA Montreal

+ *2001 Named coach of the month for April*: National Coaching Institute

+ *2002 Named coach of the month for February*: National Coaching Institute

+ *2002 Received Medal of Citizenship*: City of Deux-Montagnes in April

+ *2002 Received medal from the National Assembly in Quebec City* on April 11th

+ *2002 Received Ingenuity Award* in the name of Pierre Elliott Trudeau, Toronto, April 11th

+ *2002 Received Director's Medal*: Montreal Urban Police Department, April 15th

+ *2002 Received Dignity Award*: Grace Under pressure, CAAWS, April 16th

+ *2002 Coach of the month for April*: Club de la Medaille d'OR

+ *2002 Awarded honorary degree*: Doctor of Civil Law, Saint Mary's University, Halifax

+ *2002 Gold Medallist at the Olympic Games in Salt Lake City*

ABOUT THE AUTHOR

Sally Manning grew up on Pheasant Hollow Farm, a fifteen-acre tract of apple orchard and forest near Maple, Ontario. At that time, the farm was still very much in a country setting, and life revolved around the natural world just outside the back door. With two brothers and four sisters, there was never a problem finding playmates. Her earliest recollections centre around hockey, heading down to the pond in the hollow, skates and stick in hand, on that first frosty morning when the ice had grown just thick enough for skating. Many a winter's evening after school and Saturdays and Sundays was spent playing countless games up to "ten" against her older brother, Bob, and whoever else wanted to join the fun. Unfortunately, organized hockey was still not an option for most girls in the fifties and sixties.

In the fall of 1967, Sally began her studies at the University of Toronto. Here, she was introduced to field hockey and quickly became a stalwart on the varsity squad. In 1971, she was selected to the Canadian team, beginning a decade-long career at the national level. The highlight came in 1979 at the World Championship in Vancouver, when she was chosen to the World All-Star Team, the first Canadian ever given this honour.

Away from the pitch, Sally taught high school in York Region, north of Toronto. In 1984, she spent her first summer in Canada's North, paddling the legendary Nahanni River. She's spent every summer since sea kayaking, hiking and canoeing in Greenland, Nunavut, the Northwest Territories and the Yukon, much of the time as a guide for Black Feather, a wilderness adventure company.
In 1988, Sally was inducted into the University of Toronto

Sports Hall of Fame. This was followed by induction into the Vaughan Sports Hall of Fame in its inaugural year. Her dreams of one day playing in the NHL continue to flicker as she skates for the Parry Sound Phantoms in a four-team loop in Ontario's lake land.

She has written for several Canadian publications including *Up Here*, *Explore*, and *Doctor's Review* and one U.S. magazine, *Women in Sport*. *A Golden Tear* is her first book.